UNDERSTANDING HOW OTHERS MISUNDERSTAND YOU

Workbook

Ken Voges & Ron Braund

MOODY PRESS

CHICAGO

CONTENTS

About the Authors

Ken R. Voges (B.A.) is president of In His Grace, Inc., which provides believers and the church with behavioral tools and training. He is the author of numerous publications integrating the styles of biblical characters with the DISC model of behavior. Mr. Voges also does human resource consulting for Fortune 500 companies, nonprofit corporations, and churches.

Mr. Voges and his wife, Linda, are active in their local church where he teaches an adult Sunday School class and serves on the elder board. They have two children, Randy and Christy.

Ron L. Braund (M.E., D.Min.) is the president of AlphaCare Therapy Service, Inc., which is a growing network of Christ-centered outpatient and inpatient counseling centers based in Atlanta, Georgia. Dr. Braund is a licensed marriage and family therapist and clinical member of the American Association for Marriage and Family Therapy (AAMFT). He also serves as the executive director of the International Congress on Christian Counseling, which provides a forum for the ongoing integration of theology and psychology among mental health professionals and pastors.

In addition to his clinical work, he is president of the Institute for Leadership Development (ILD) offering consultation and training to universities, corporations, and churches across America.

Dr. Braund and his wife, Ginger, have two children, Rich and Adam.

Foreword

I first met Ken Voges when I was a pastor in Houston, Texas, in the mid-1970s. Early in our friendship I shared a few insights with him and his wife, Linda, concerning temperament differences and their effect on marriage relationships. Finding these ideas personally helpful, Ken soon began to pursue studies in the area with diligence and tenacity.

First reading on the subject of personality theory, then attempting to teach classes on the subject, then discovering the instruments developed by the Performax, then studying biblical biographies in depth with the help of able exegesis, and by repeatedly testing those conclusions in group settings and in personal counseling, then, after more than fifteen years of study and teaching, Ken and Dr. Ron Braund have produced a book and workbook that thoroughly correlate analyses of temperament types with data on biblical personalities.

Other books and resource materials have been on temperament differences, but this study is unique. The reader will be impressed with four major distinctives. First, the study is directly correlated with well respected instruments for measuring four key temperament traits. Second, Ken and Ron have presented a large number of biblical personalities among which the reader can find one similar to himself or herself. Third, the focus of the book and workbook is directed toward the development of loving environments for others. And fourth, the pages are enriched with numerous personal examples.

Because Ken has been a great help to me personally over the years and because Dr. Braund offers a valuable perspective as a licensed marriage and family therapist, I am especially excited over the publication of these volumes. They have provided insights helpful to me in my relationship with my family and in solving management problems that I have faced as a pastor, university president, and Campus Crusade for Christ team player.

I commend the Voges and Braund book and workbook, _Understanding How Others Misunderstand You_, as interesting and helpful personal reading and as a useful guide for group study, especially when used in conjunction with the biblical instrument.

JOE L. WALL Th.D.
Coordinator of Church Planter Training
for Campus Crusade for Christ and
Director of Church Planting
East-West Ministries International

Preface

Some 20 years ago, I (Ken) was introduced to a behavioral model that identified different personality styles. It was extremely helpful to my wife Linda and me in understanding that differences are normal. Up until that time we were doing what many others married couples were practicing.....trying to change our partners to be like us. It wasn't working.

These new concepts helped us accept one another as we began viewing differing styles as strengths rather than weaknesses. Shortly thereafter, I began teaching adult Sunday school classes, integrating some of this information into my presentations. The reactions were generally positive. Participants began to focus on personal needs and to accept personality differences as being normal. New levels of understanding developed for most. Unfortunately, greater insight created for others a potential for misuse. Some class members used the information as an excuse for their behavior and even labeled others with negative tags.

This development disturbed me because I knew the information had much positive potential, if presented properly. I felt the key to overcoming the problem had to be in using the Scriptures alongside the material. I began to analyze the behavior of personalities found in Scripture. That became a useful approach for helping others to associate their behavior with positive biblical models. The main focus of my teaching shifted to the Scriptures, which also helped overcome negative uses of the information.

In 1979, Betty Bowman introduced me to Dr. John Geier's DISC model of behavior and the instrument he developed. I spent the next five years testing these concepts against the unique behavioral styles of biblical characters. It was a fascinating study. The characters came alive from the pages of Scriptures. I was given the opportunity to modify the secular instrument to include biblical characters, and in 1984 a *biblical instrument* was published. Currently over 200,000 instruments have been used with church groups, in counseling sessions, and for staff team building. In 1990, I left the General Electric Company to begin writing the <u>Understanding</u> series for Moody Press. I continually am encouraged to see the positive benefits others experienced as they discover how to love one another.

One afternoon in 1985, I (Ron) was talking with Bruce Edwards, the youth minister of a church our counseling organization serves in Atlanta, Georgia. He showed me a copy of Ken's *biblical instrument*. As a licensed marriage and family therapist, I had used several assessment tools with clients in order to help understand their personalities. I had even developed a seminar using a temperament analysis as the foundation for improving communication. Upon exploring an instrument integrated with biblical characters, I recognized it as an available tool for helping people to understand one another.

This version of the DISC material gave insight into how others are motivated and into how misunderstanding tends to surface between people. Relating different behavioral styles to personalities like Peter, Paul, Moses, and Abraham provided powerful metaphors for integrating biblical truth with psychological principles.

After I experienced Ken's instrument, I desired to know more. Ken invited me to meet with him, and several weeks later I flew to Houston and received training from Ken and met his lovely wife, Linda. Out of that experience, a close working relationship developed. Since that time, I have traveled throughout the United States training others in the integration of DISC with biblical principle and working with Ken to develop additional materials. We have different behavioral styles and have had the opportunity to apply the truths contained in this book.

Our study of this material has revealed that God of the Bible is for a more personal than we had ever realized. He clearly understands the needs of each one of us and modeled the way to understand and love one another rather than to react and reject one another. The purpose of this workbook—and the book that it accompanies—is to help you understand how others may be misunderstanding you and to help you relate your unique behavioral style to a positive biblical character. This discovery can reinforce in your thinking the truth that God has a special purpose for your life. In addition, our desire is that you will be able to devise specific love strategies for improving the quality of relationships with your partner, your children, your friends, and your associates. Your reward will be to experience personal fulfillment and to become more effective in serving Christ.

RECOGNIZING DIFFERENCES

Assignment:
Understanding How Others Misunderstand You,
textbook chapter 1, pages 15-31

What's the purpose of this study?

The purpose of this session is twofold: to introduce ways to recognize differences in personality styles among people and to discover your own personality style by taking the DISC biblical instrument. The workbook and the textbook that accompanies it are based on the idea that God gave each of us a unique cluster of behavioral characteristics. Those behavioral characteristics include a set of distinct needs. When we recognize what our own needs are we will be better able to understand and meet the needs of others.

Unfortunately, personality differences often become barriers to accepting one other and living out the biblical command to show unconditional love. Identifying and understanding diversity among personality profiles is a big step in learning how to cooperate with others instead of struggling with ineffective communication.

What Makes Us Different?

We often assume that others think the way we do. But they don't. Similary. we often assume that we know what accounts for the differences we do notice. But we don't. Respond to the first set of questions below individually. Then share your answers with your partner or, if you are completing this workbook as part of a seminar, with the other members of your discussion group.

When you have completed your discussion, move on to the second set of questions. As you do, think about the differences in personality the questions reveal.

On the answer blanks, indicate your agreement or disagreement with the following statements. Then discuss your reasons for making the choices you did.

1. Men have different expectations for personal relationships than do women. *Yes. Men: Help, having fun together, loyalty* *Women: Support, intimacy, understanding*

2. Women have different emotions than do men. *No. Definitely different ways of expressing them. Possibly different degrees.*

3. Individuals who are committed Christians will have fewer conflicts in their personal relationships than those who are not. *Not fewer conflicts, but should be more capable of working them out in a positive manner.*

4. People who yield in conflicts demonstrate Christian love. *Depends on why they yield. Not necessarily.*

5. A woman who finds it necessary to clarify her needs to her husband and tell him how to meet those needs is married to a man who is insensitive and lacking in perception. *No. He's normal.*

Choose one of the following by circling your preference.

1. Do you see yourself as being more **extroverted** or **introverted**?
2. If you see yourself as an extrovert, are you more **goal-oriented** and **direct** toward others or more **people-oriented** and **relational** toward others?
3. If you see yourself as an **introvert**, do you tend to be more a **supporter** of others or more concerned for **details and facts**?
4. When you are under stress, do you tend to **vent your feelings** or do you **suppress your feelings**?
5. As you approach a task, do you prefer to **start the process** and **delegate** others to do the details or you prefer to **follow through** and **finish** a task until completed.

Differences in Perception

Differences in behavioral style among people are related to more fundamental differences in perception, motivation, needs, and values. **Look at the drawing of the glass and place a check mark beside the response at the right that best matches your description of it.**

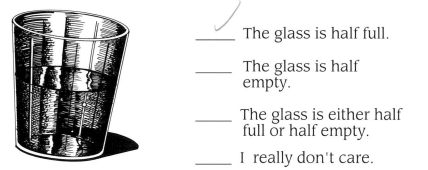

√ The glass is half full.

_____ The glass is half empty.

_____ The glass is either half full or half empty.

_____ I really don't care.

Some people see the glass in terms of fullness and some see it in terms of emptiness; but strickly speaking, all four responses are accurate. For what is being asked for in this instance is a person's initial response to the glass. All four responses can be normal within a group. In fact, the danger to the personality lies in denying people the right to an honest, candid reaction to what they see.

This difference among people in what they see when they look at the glass is a difference of perception. It is one of the factors that make up a person's unique personality style.

Differences in Motivation

When it comes to understanding motivation, it is important to distinquish between how a person is motivated and the environment he needs for that motivation to occur. The following statements explain general principles related to motivation.

1. You cannot motivate other people.
2. However, all people are motivated.
3. People are motivated for their own reasons and necessarily your reasons.
4. The very best you can do to motivate others is to create an environment which allows individuals to motivate themselves.

What motivates you might not motivate someone else. The questions below will help you begin to discover the environment you need if you are to be truly motivated.

Describe what is motivating for you:

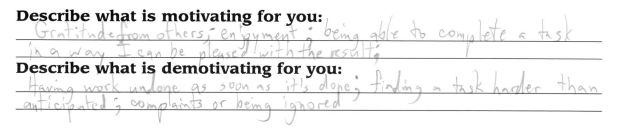

Gratitude from others; enjoyment; being able to complete a task in a way I can be pleased with the result;

Describe what is demotivating for you:

Having work undone as soon as it's done; finding a task harder than anticipated; complaints or being ignored

Overview of the DISC System

Table 1, DISC Overview, identifies the distinctive characteristics of the four DISC personality styles and shows how they are related to one another. It also shows how each personality style reacts to the different environments, what they are likely to emphasize in a given situation, and the goals they characteristically have. Which style best describes you.

DISC Overview

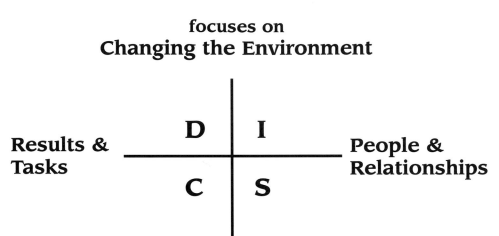

Table 1

A Dominance style tends to prefer an environment that allows them to be in control and create results.

An Influencing style tends to prefer an environment that allows social interaction.

A Steadiness style tends to prefer an environment that is stable and secure.

A Compliance style tends to prefer an environment that places a high value on being right and safe.

High and Low DISC Styles

In each DISC continuum, circle the high or low style that best describes you.

Continuums	High Styles:	Low Styles:
D's Dominance	Most comfortable working independently, tend to focus on achieving results.	Most comfortable working as a part of a team, tend to focus on achieving team goals.
I's Influencing	Most comfortable working with and around people, tend to focus on building and maintaining relationships.	Most comfortable working alone, tend to focus on analyzing data and coming to logical conclusions.
S's Steadiness	Most comfortable working in a structured, routine setting; tend to focus on maintaining harmony in the work place.	Most comfortable working in a flexible, unstructured environment; tend focus on creating varied activities.
C's Compliance	Most comfortable working in a clearly defined system, tend to focus on doing things right and maintaining accuracy.	Most comfortable working with no defined system, tend to be free-spirited, and focus on being in control of the environment.

Why We Need to Learn about
Needs-motivated Behavior

Learning about DISC needs-motivated behavior is necessary to better meet the needs of others and in turn fulfill Christ's commandment in Matthew 22:34-40 (italics added):

> Hearing that Jesus had silenced the Sadduces, the Pharisees got together. One of them, an expert in the law, tested Him with this question: "Teacher, which is the greatest commandment in the Law?" Jesus replied: "' *Love the Lord your God with all your heart and with all your soul and with all your mind.'* This is the first and greatest commandment. And the second is like it: *'Love your neighbor as yourself.'*" All the Law and the Prophets hang on these two commandments.

Jesus' response, which quoted Deuteronomy 6:5 and Leviticus 19:18, emphasized a personal relationship with God as being the most important (v. 37), and the relationship between ourselves and anyone who comes into our area of influence (v. 39) as being the next in importance. The word Jesus used for love was *agapao*, which refers to a level of love that is both self-sacrificing and attached to meeting the needs of others. Jesus' position was that if you practiced these two commands, all other laws would be fulfilled.

Christ's second commandment, "Love your neighbor as yourself," expresses a great truth about human relationships. If you sacrifice yourself without taking care of your own needs, you will have nothing of quality left to give to others. The only way we can ever love others in a self-sacrificial way is by first having a clear understanding of ourselves and how to take care of our own needs (physical, emotional, and spiritual). When we have a grasp of those needs we will be capable of serving the needs of others.

The DISC model used in this workbook and the accompanying textbook is a tool you can use to get a better idea of what your own needs are and how they can best be met. It will also help you understand the needs of others and what you can do to meet their needs.

> "You shall love your neighbor as yourself"
> means
> meeting others' needs
> in concert with meeting your own needs.

Summing it up: The DISC model measures _____needs_____ and is intended to be used as a tool to help you fulfill Christ's command.

A Look Ahead

Now that you have been introduced to DISC, you are ready to discover your own unique style of behavior.

ASSESSING YOUR DISC STYLE

Assignment:
Understanding How Others Misunderstand You,
textbook chapter 2, pages 33-52

To determine your DISC pattern you will need to turn page 117 and begin the self assessment process. A second assessment is also available on page 147. Regarding your style, keep in mind the following principles:

1. There are no better or worse profiles in this instrument.
2. We all have individual strengths, weaknesses, and areas in which we need to grow.
3. Successful people are those who
    *   understand themselves and how they tend to affect other people;
    *   can identify their own strengths and weaknesses without being defensive;
    *   have developed the ability to be flexible and adjust their behavior style in order to meet the needs of a specific situation or to relate to people with different profiles.

Guidelines for understanding
your DISC style

The purpose of the DISC instrument is to help you understand yourself and others. It features a self-interpreting process involving four stages. Below is a brief explanation of the four stages and how to proceed in the self-interpreting process.

1. General highlights of the DISC model (pages 120,122-123).
2. DISC strengths and weaknesses (page 124-125).
3. Association with Biblical model (page 134).
4. Association with a representative profile pattern (pages 135-143).

Phase 1: General highlights (pages 120, 122-123)
1. Turn to page 119 or 149 and circle all plotting points above the mid line on Graphs III. Turn to page 134 or 151 and determine your representative high styles and biblical character.
2. Turn to pages 122-123 and focus on the DISC styles that correspond to your highest plotting points(s). Underline the descriptive phrases that are accurate of you.
3. Mark through those phrases that do not describe you.

Phase 2: DISC Strengths and Weaknesses (page 124-131)
1. Turn to page 124 and complete the assignments as outlined.
2. Determine the accuracy of the circled words as they relate to your behavior.

Phase 3: Association with biblical model (page 132-134)
1. Turn to page 133 and circle the DISC blends that represent your DISC styles above the midline in Graphs III **(Composite Graph)**.
2. Circle the biblical character that corresponds to your circled styles.
3. Look up the biblical references and determine if the biblical character parallels your behavior.

Phase 4: Association with a Representative Profile Pattern (pages 135-143)
1. Turn to page 134 or 151 and circle your representative pattern among the 16 DISC styles.
2. Find your Representative Profile and underline words or phases that describe you.

Using the DISC Continuum
to Profile Biblical Characters

The DISC Continuum was the means used to develop the Scripture parallels for the DISC representative profiles patterns. Turn to the next page of this workbook and complete the exercise in profiling the behavior of the Apostle Peter.

Profiling the behavior
of the Apostle Peter

WHERE DOES THE SCRIPTURE SPEAK ABOUT PERSONAL PROFILES ?

II Timothy 3

16 All Scripture is inspired by God and profitable for teaching, for reproof, for correction, for training in righteousness;

17 that the man of God may be adequate, equipped for every good work.

Purpose:

This exercise will help you understand how to correlate behavior traits to characters in the Bible.

Scripture teaches us about God and the way He works in and through many different kinds of people. Peter was different from Paul. Moses was different from David. Mary was different from Martha.

Different as they were, each was used by God in ways unique to their style.. Notice, though, that He used them in different ways and in different places. What's more, He showed His divine love in different ways. Likewise, the body of Christ is made up of different people.

To profile scripture characters:

1. **Focus** on the passages that describe **people's behavior.**
2. **Accept** the recorded **bibilcal account as accurate.**
3. **List any specific traits** that describe these characters or their actions and associate them with the words on the DISC continuums.
4. **Determine whether these traits cluster** on the four DISC continuums into a definable profile.

Peter:
A Behavioral Case Study

Your assignment is to read Matthew 14:22-33 and focus on Peter's actions in verses 28-30 and describe what he did.

Matthew 14:22-33

28 And Peter answered Him and said, "Lord, if it is You, command me to come to You on the water."

29 And He said, "Come!" And Peter got out of the boat, and walked on the water and came toward Jesus.

30 But seeing the wind, he became afraid, and beginning to sink, he cried out, saying, "Lord, save me!"

Assignment: Look at the three traits in each of the following four continuums and place a **circle** around the **words in each group** that best describes Peter's behavior.

D **Decisive** risk-taker   I   Acting out of **trust**
     Calculated risk-taker   Acting out of **reflection**
     Conservative risk-taker   Acting out of **logic**

S   Being a **team player**   C   **Systematic**
     Being **alert**   **Analytical**
     Being **spontaneous**   **Independent**

Based on your selections put the terms together in a sentence to describe what he did.

Peter was an *independent, spontaneous risk-taker acting out of trust*

Based on your choice find the trait that you selected on the DISC continuum on the opposite page. Do the traits immediately above and below the words you selected describe what Peter did?

DISC Trait Continuums

High D Dominance **Comfortable working independently**	High I Influence **Comfortable working with people**	High S Steadiness **Comfortable working in a routine**	High C Compliance **Comfortable working in a defined system**
driving belligerent domineering dictatorial pioneering	charismatic persuasive spontaneous emotional glib	patient loyal steady **team player** indifferent	perfectionistic accurate diplomatic **systematic** precise
adventuresome decisive **risk-taker** takes chances curious self-assured hasty	trusts others overly optimistic gullible agreeable sociable pleasant charitable	cooperative kind too lenient remaining still at ease good listener nonemotional	worrisome thorough conscientious restrained **analytical** conforms to rules critical of self
competitive confident positive	confident optimistic poor listener	deliberate amiable dependable	sensitive compliant too compliant
hesitant **calculates risks** self-critical	convincing prefers harmony adaptable	mobile **alert** restless	self-confident "own person" expresses opinion
unassuming discounts self realistic **conservative** willing shy peaceful	**reflective** reserved factual suspicious nonemotional reflective aloof	responsive ready and willing critical of others flexible impatient active restless	firm persistent **independent** unconventional determined strong-willed immovable
humble nondemanding fearful dependent meek	pessimistic **logical** withdrawn detached probing	energetic intense **spontaneous** dynamic hyperactive	defiant rebellious free-spirited fearless sarcastic
Comfortable working on a team **Low D** Dominance	**Comfortable working alone** **Low I** Influence	**Comfortable working with no structure** **Low S** Steadiness	**Comfortable working with no system** **Low C** Compliance

Peter:
A DISC Behavioral Case Study

Under either positve or negative **stress,** a High D will become aggressive; a High I prefers to talk and entertain friends, a High S prefers having time to process, and High C desires to validate and be alone. Read Matthew 17:1-5 and determine what Peter did. What style did he emulate?

A **strength** of a High D is to create action; a High I, to articulate his thoughts and the thoughts of others; the High S to follow through and maintain the status quo, and the High C, to cautiously analyze data. Read Matthew 16:13-20 and explain Peter's actions and relate them to a particular style of behavior.

Strengths out of control can become a person's greatest weakness. The High D can create action when it is not needed, whereas a High I can express his opinion when it is unappropriate. The High S can maintain the status quo when action is needed, whereas the High C can spend time analyzing data that is unimportant. Read Matthew 16:21-23. What style does Peter represent in this passage?

In a **favorable environment**, the I/D style confidently believes he can positively impact any situation. The S/C style remains cautious and uncommitted until he has time to process the information. Read Matthew 26:30-33, Luke 22:31-33, and Matthew 26:34-35. Describe Peter's actions in these passages. Which style does he represent?

In an **unfavorable environment**, the I/D style tends to respond emotionally to events and forget past commitments. S/C will remember what commitments were made and followthrough. Read Matthew 26:57-75 and John 19:26-27. Describe what happened. What style does Peter represent and what style does John represent?

Identifying Your Profile Style
and Biblical Character

       Research has shown that no more than twenty percent of the population is identified as having behavioral tendencies that are "pure" DISC styles. For most of us, more than one DISC trait significantly influences our personality makeup. The profile styles in the biblical instrument offer a more precise level of interpretation. They identify sixteen of the most commonly occurring combinations of DISC traits.

       Once you have identified your pattern or style, you can also select the biblical character of your choosing that the Scripture indicates closely resembles your unique behavioral style.

DISC Exercise

1. The profile or style I most relate to is the _____analyst_____ because the following traits are also true of me:

    reliable, factual, steady cooperative, painstakingly accurate, diplomatic, avoids unnecessary trouble, sensitive to hidden meanings & ulterior motives

2. The biblical character I most identify with is _____Moses_____ because:

    of need to have everything clear & certain & well understood, then willing to follow through patiently. Wanting clear orders.

    ☆ Should follow up on possibility of identifying with Naomi, too.

A Look Ahead

       Now that you have identified your unique personality style, you are ready to begin learning how your tendencies compare and contrast with others. This discovery will help you see how misunderstanding often develops between people with different behavioral styles.

UNDERSTANDING EXPECTATIONS AND ENVIRONMENTS

Assignment:
Understanding How Others Misunderstand You,
textbook chapter 3, pages 53-68

In order to build relationships, we must understand and respect differences as normal. Misunderstandings often occur when we think people should respond in ways consistent with our own natural responses. The purpose of this session is to identify how different expectations affect how we relate to one another.

Efforts to change one another rather than accept one another frequently lead to disagreements. The Golden Rule states, "Do unto others as you would like others to do unto you." This principle has helped guide us in treating our fellow man with more respect. One way to foster acceptance and minimize conflicts is to treat others the way we would like to be treated.

Understanding Differences in DISC Expectations

(The number 10 indicates high expectations; the number 0, low expectations)

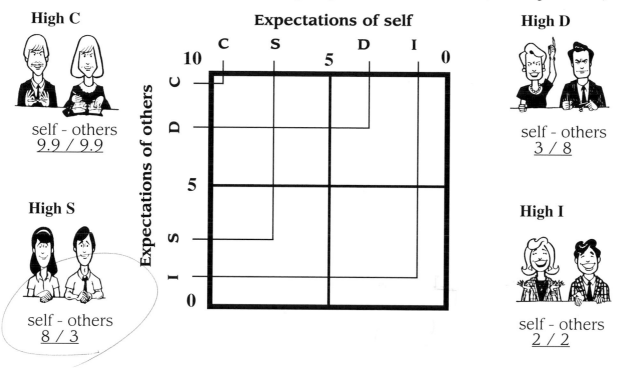

High C

self - others
9.9 / 9.9

High S

self - others
8 / 3

High D

self - others
3 / 8

High I

self - others
2 / 2

Exercise A: Read the following and discuss the difference between the expectations of the two individuals.

Bill has agreed to meet Gene for a business lunch. Bill arrives ten minutes early in order to beat the crowd and get a table. He tells the waitress that he will order when his partner arrives. Now consider Bill's thoughts when it is fifteen minutes past the time Gene agreed to meet.

It has been twenty minutes, and Gene's late again. I don't think he has ever been on time. I should have known and been late myself, but I just can't do that. Now the waitress is annoyed at me because I have taken up a table too long. I feel embarassed--no, I feel angry. I bet Gene will have an excuse--he always does. Now he is thirty minutes late. Should I just leave? I can't believe he is so inconsiderate.

About this time, Gene drives up and rushes through the door. Listen to his thoughts.

Great. Bill hasn't left. I bet he's making good use of his time--he always does. That last phone call I got before leaving the office made me late, but it was very important. My customer was upset that he had not received his order, and I needed to smooth his feathers. Everything is fine now, and I even got the man to place another order for our new product line. Oh well, I have the rest of the afternoon free and can spend as much time as I need with Bill.

As Gene gets to the table, he says, "Hi, Bill. Sorry I am a little late. Things got busy at the office all of a sudden. Can we order now and then get down to business?

1.   We can see that Bill and Gene have a different perspective of what is important concerning being on time for the lunch appointment. Which of the four DISC profiles is most characteristic of Bill? ____C____ What about Gene ? ____I____

2.   What were the different expectations of each man?

B - important to be on time

G - unimportant " " "

3.   How could this problem be avoided on another occasion?

Bill lower expectations, relax, or Gene call about being late.

Exercise B. Suppose you agreed to a 12:00 noon luncheon with a friend. Look at the chart highlighting the expectations of the different DISC styles. Describe what each profile would expect of himself and of you.

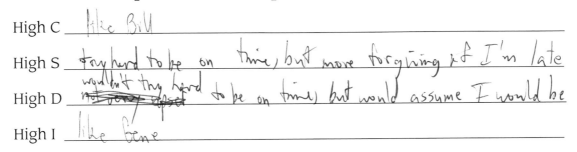

High C _like Bill_

High S _try hard to be on time, but more forgiving if I'm late_

High D _wouldn't try hard to be on time, but would assume I would be_

High I _like Gene_

Understanding DISC Environments

Behavior consultants have identified a modification of the Golden Rule. It is called the "Platinum Rule." The Platinum Rule is designed to increase our ability to relate to others. It states,"Do unto others the way they prefer to be done unto." In others words, if we learn how to treat others in a manner that is consistent with the environment within which they respond best, then we can move closer toward achieving harmony and understanding. Understanding DISC environments involves developing our ability to respond to another person in a way that is consistent with his preferences.

On the opposite page is a breakdown of the key verbs found in I Thessalonians 5:14. This passage offers a biblical framework to study the different types environments one could choose in responding to others.

On page 30 is a template on creating specific environments for the D-I-S-C styles. Apply this information in both these pages as you work your way through the exercises on page 31, paying particular attention to the way you can "meet another person halfway" in your dealings with him by creating an environment in which he can flourish.

Differences in Scriptural Environments

*"And we **urge** you, brethren, **admonish** the unruly, **encourage** the fainthearted, **help** the weak, **be patient** with all men."*

I Thessalonians 5:14

Biblical verb	Meaning	Type Environment
urge *(Parakaleo)*	beseech or exhort (mildly active)	urgency to listen and respond to a directive
admonish *(Nouthetheo)*	to warn, to confront to produce a change in lifestyle. (very active)	intended to create a confrontation for the purpose of producing a change in direction or behavior
encourage *(Parmutheomai)*	console, comfort and cheerup (active)	includes elements of understanding and redirecting of thoughts and focus from negative to positive
help *(Antechanai)*	taking interest in, rendering assistance, holding up spiritually and emotionally (passive)	involves coming along-side of a person and supporting him
patience *(Makrothumeo)*	to be long-tempered to express patience (passive)	involves projecting encouragement and goodwill

Building DISC Relationships

DOMINANCE (D)

[handwritten: Doug Aaron Russell]

HOW TO RESPOND TO A HIGH D
- Be firm and direct
- Focus on actions and goals
- Caring confrontation may be necessary to get his attention

HOW TO RELATE TO A HIGH D
- Be brief and to the point
- Explain "How to achieve goals" using logic with an action plan
- Allow time to consider your ideas

HOW TO REINFORCE THE HIGH D
- Repeat the plan of action focusing on goals, objectives, and results
- Give bottomline instructions
- Get out of his way

INFLUENCING (I)

[handwritten: Aaron]

HOW TO RESPOND TO A HIGH I
- Be friendly and positive
- Allow for informal dialogue
- Allow time for stimulating and fun activities

HOW TO RELATE TO A HIGH I
- Use friendly voice tones
- Allow time for them to verbalize their feelings
- You transfer talk to an action plan

HOW TO REINFORCE THE HIGH I
- Offer positive encouragement and incentives for taking on tasks
- You organize the action plan
- Communicate positive recognition

COMPLIANCE (C)

HOW TO RESPOND TO A HIGH C
- Be specific and accurate
- Make allowance for initial responses to be cautious and/or negative
- Allow freedom to ask questions

HOW TO RELATE TO A HIGH C
- Answer questions in a patient and persistent manner
- Mix accurate data with assurances
- Allow time to validate information

HOW TO REINFORCE THE HIGH C
- Provide a step by approach to a goal
- Provide reassurances of support
- Give permission to validate information with third parties

STEADINESS (S)

[handwritten: Peggy Russell]

HOW TO RESPOND TO A HIGH S
- Be nonthreatening and patient
- Allow time to process and adjust to change
- Make allowances for family

HOW TO RELATE TO A HIGH S
- Use friendly tones when instructing
- Give personal, nonverbal acceptance and assurances
- Allow time to process information

HOW TO REINFORCE THE HIGH S
- Repeat any instructions
- Provide hands-on reinforcement
- Be patient in allowing time to take ownership

Used by permission of In His Grace,Inc.

26

1. Let's suppose you were attempting to market a new product to a customer. While he talks with you on the phone he asks many specific details and requests that you make a formal presentation. What do you suspect his profile is and how would you prepare for this appointment?

   High C - prepare in detail, be ready to answer all questions
   and provide assurances, prepare a proper, very formal presentation,
   but don't press too hard for an immediate response.

2. In your own words describe the major environmental differences of the :

   High D _goal- and bottom-line- oriented_

   High I _personal reaction - oriented_

   High S _assimilation- oriented_

   High C _information- oriented_

3. Which of the five words mentioned in I Thessalonians 5:14 are most comforting to you when you are under stress: urge, admonish, encourage, help, or patience? Explain why. _patience; I would like to be able to work through_
   it myself, just need room to do so. Encouragement also comforting.

4. Look again at the DISC environments chart. Select the phrases in the chart that are most important for others to consider when they relate to you.

   patience, allowing time
   nonthreatening, acceptance, assurance
   accurate information,
   specific

A Look Ahead

Knowing what the DISC personalities expect and the environments in which they flourish will give you a solid foundation for helping to resolve misunderstanding. Now we can look at everyday situations and anticipate what reactions to expect from the different DISC styles.

THE DISC PERSONALITY STYLES
IN DAILY LIVING

Assignment:
Understanding How Others Misunderstand You,
textbook, chapter 4, pages 69-77

We can better understand one another if we know what reactions to expect from the four DISC personality styles in everyday life. If one picture is worth a thousand words, then a group of portraits will speak volumes. The claims of this proverb will come alive in this session as we use cartoons to help characterize our understanding of the differing ways each of us tends to respond to a similar set of circumstances.

<u>Cartoons That Characterize Our Differences</u>

An artist, Dan Dunn, has captured the distinctive qualities of the four DISC personalities in a series of cartoons. These cartoons will give you a shorthand way of keeping in mind the distinct characteristics of the four DISC personalities. That, in turn, will help you predict what you can expect from other persons. We ask that you not take the characterizations presented in the cartoons too personally. All of us need to loosen up and laugh at ourselves at the same time we are learning how to understand one another. We recommend that before you attempt to fit yourself into any one category, consider the fact that we all have a blending of several DISC styles. Each of us is unique. The cartoons only highlight the extreme traits manifested by the personality styles.

Before you review the pictures of the various DISC styles, there are some ground rules that have to be respected.

DISC Ground Rules

Even though labels are a natural part of describing people, places, and things, inappropriate use of labels can be dangerous. If a label helps clarify differences, then it is useful. But if the label creates barriers, it can be harmful. At this point in your understanding of the DISC descriptions, the following ground rules will help you exercise caution in applying the DISC personality profiles to your daily life.

Ground Rules

Don't nudge

Don't pigeon-hole

Don't label others

Don't flaunt your knowledge

**Don't use your knowledge
as an excuse**

Bible is final authority

30

The High D (Dominant) cartoon is the one at the left. Notice that he has a more intense, no nonsense look, as well as being more direct. The High I (Influencing is at the top left center. This man is a bit more causal, with an outgoing look on his face indicating the tendency toward openness and friendliness. The High S (Steadiness) is at the right center. He has a more conservative look and is intent on being supportive. Finally, the High C (Cautious) is at the right. he is characterized as an intense thinker and someone who is more cautious and analytical. With these pictures in mind, let us look at the way these personality styles react to different situations in life.

The DISC Personality Styles in Daily Living

The four DISC personality styles have characteristically different responses to various situations.Turn to chapter 4 in *Understanding How Others Misunderstand You* textbook (pp. 69-77), and read the material in conjunction with the cartoons that appear on pages 32-38 of this workbook chapter.

Approach to Teamwork

High D:
- initiates action
- takes charge
- moves out to reach a goal

High I:
- draws upon contacts to gather the resources needed for the project

High S:
- ensures follow through
- offers support

High C:
- offers design, technical and quality control

High D

High I

High S

High C

Leadership or Management Style

High D:
- adopts an autocratic style
- defines responsibilities
- implements action plans with accountability

High I:
- adopts a democratic style
- facilitates open communication with others
- desires consensus before making final decisions

High S:
- adopts a participative style
- listens and follows through
- strives for peace and harmony

High C:
- adopts a bureaucratic style
- emphasizes quality and procedures
- desires compliance to written standards

High D

High I

High S

High C

33

Sensitivity to Feelings of Others

High D:
- tends to be insensitive to the feelings of others
- sees emotional expressions as obstacles
- sees life as a battle

High I:
- is more sensitive to others
- wants others to be happy
- is quick to offer encouragement and reach out to others

High S:
- conscious of feelings
- tries to avoid hurting
- avoids conflict and stirring up controversy

High C:
- task oriented
- takes a logical, analytical approach to feelings
- sees things as black and white

High D

High I

High S

High C

Releasing Stress

High D: • becomes intense when goals are blocked
• prone to fits of anger
• relieves stress through physical exercise

Doug Aaron Russell

High I: • becomes more talkative
• prone to verbal attacks
• seeks social gatherings

High S: • avoids conflict
• tends to internalize stress
• releases stress by sleeping

Kathy Peggy

High C: • dislikes disorganization
• prone to become critical
• desires to be alone in times of stress

High D

High I

High S

High C

Recovery from Emotional Stress

High D: • by taking time to engage in physical activity

High S: • by taking time to do non threatening, routine activities (watching TV)

High I: • by socially spending time with others
• talking on the phone

High C: • by having private time away from people (reading books)
• by being alone

High D

High I

High S

High C

Making a Spiritual Commitment to Christ

High D: • often through a traumatic event which challenges his control over his life and future

High S: • often through a *process* of logical thinking of who Jesus is

High I: • often through an inspiring presentaion of the gospel requiring a public commitment

High C: • often through realization that only Jesus has the answer to their *felt* guilt

High D

High I

High S

High C

Being the Pastor of a Church

High D:
- drives the church to provide programs for all people
- takes an aggressive, goal-oriented approach

High S:
- prefers a traditional church
- works toward peace and harmony

High I:
- focus on programs that satisfy peoples' needs
- services are often doctrine over grace

High C:
- prefers a church that operates "by the book"
- tends to emphasize unique and expressive

High D

High I

High S

High C

DISCovery Worksheet

In order to further discover the uniqueness of your profile, respond to each of the statements below.

1. When I looked at the cartoons, I related best to the one that: *showed S responding to religion as logical.*

2. I would describe my leadership style to be: *Definitely high S*

3. I feel I have value to the team because I can: *keep in touch with everyone's needs & personal goals while trying to stick with the plan & major goal.*

4. I tend to handle stress by: *sleeping (!)*

5. I recover from emotional stress by: *reading (high C), being away & alone*

A Look Ahead

By now you should have a general understanding of what to expect from each one of the DISC personality styles. The eight sessions that follow will take an in-depth look at each of the four main behavior patterns.

UNDERSTANDING THE DOMINANCE STYLE

Assignment:

Understanding How Others Misunderstand You,
textbook chapter 5 pages 79-100

Τhe **Dominance** or **High D** individual is direct, confident, and straightforward. The High D loves challenges, and it only inspires him to action when others caution, "It cannot be done." High D's focus principally on goals and tasks. Frequently, the High D see people only as a means to accomplish a goal. Whereas, the High D and C are likely to view events with an antagonistic focus, the High I and High S are likely to focus on harmony and on creating a favorable, friendly environment.

We will focus in this lesson on how the Dominance styles work and how they relate to the others personality patterns in the other three profiles. In addition, we will discuss the ways the High D is likely to be misunderstood by others. Our goal will be to gain awareness of why conflicts with the Dominance personality style occur and what can be done to work through those issues to build solid relationships.

Finally, we will learn the basic tendencies of the four representative patterns in the High D family: **Pure D, D/ I, D equal I, and D/C.** We will also discover what biblical characters that represent each of these High D patterns.

Understanding High D Tendencies and Skills

Basic Tendencies

1. High D's have a high sense of personal worth, or *high ego strength*.

2. High D's are *task-oriented* and *need results*.

3. High D's are motivated by *directness*.

4. The basic fear of High D's is to be *taken advantage of*.

5. The basic blind spot for High D's is that he *lacks concern for the feelings and views of others*.

Basic Strengths

The High D possesses many dynamic strengths. However, when a High D's tendencies are out of control, they can offend others by being too aggressive and by being insensitive to the feelings of others. To counterbalance these tendencies, a High D needs to have individuals around him who have strengths that are complementary to his. Below are examples of High D strengths and the corresponding balancing strength in other profiles. Notice that in the last column, the final three complementary profiles have been left out. Which profiles best represent the complementary strength?

Strength of the High D profile	Complementary strengths needed	Patterns who have the complementary strength
Initiating	Taking care of the details	C
Decisive	Showing patience	S
Goal-oriented	Showing concern for people	I
Authoritative	Diplomatic	I
Competitive	Team player	S
Forceful	Verbalize feeling of others	I

Understanding How the High D Relates to Others

The following compatibility chart identifies the natural manner in which a Dominance person generally relates to each DISC behavioral style in social relationships and in job tasks.

Profile Teams	Excellent Chemistry			Requires Effort				Constant Work		
	10	9	8	7	6	5	4	3	2	1
D - D			R				T			
D - I		R					T			
D - S	T						R			
D - C							T		R	

KEY

R = Social Relationships
T = Job Tasks

10 = Best Possible
1 = Poorest Possible

Definitions

D - D Team: High D's respect and admire others who are action-oriented. Consequently, they often carry a personal high regard for other High D, because both are committed to results. However, because of their high ego strength, D's frequently encounter difficulty in working together because they cannot agree on who should lead or follow in achieving mutual goals.

D - I Team: High I's have the relational skills that High D's need and admire. High I's are also action-oriented, which complements the High D's need for variety. The relationships between the two can become strained because the High D has a need to control, whereas the High I has a desire to be free of structure and control.

D - S Team: High D's work well with High S's because the D's generally provide the start-up energy, whereas the S's are committed to making sure the work is completed. High D's prefer leading and High S's generally prefer following. The personal relationship between the two often suffers because High D's desire change and variety, whereas the High S's desire status quo.

D - C Team: The work relationship between D and C is difficult at times because the C is committed to maintaining structure and the status quo, whereas the D will inter-ject change as a mode of operation. The personal relationships between the two suffer because the High D is direct and confrontational, whereas the High C is extremely sensitive to criticism and withdraws from it.

Misunderstanding the HIGH D

Study the characteristics below and circle the traits that, in your opinion, could tend to lead to misunderstandings.

Characteristics of the High D

1. Dominance Tendencies include:
   solving problems,
   causing action,
   making quick decisions.

2. Desires an environment with:
   power and authority,
   activities which challenge status quo,
   brief and direct answers.

3. Judges others by:
   ability to meet their standards ,
   aggressiveness,
   quickness in accomplishing goals.

Characteristics of the other DISC styles

Tendencies of other DISC styles:
High I styles - entertaining people
High S styles - staying in one place
High C styles - concentrating on details

Desires an environment with:
High I styles - favorable working conditions
High S styles - security of the situation
High C styles - many patient explanations

Judges others by:
High I styles - verbal expression & flexibility
High S styles - consistency & getting along
High C styles - commitment to precise
                         standards

Exploring excerise:

1. Study each of the three High D characteristics and compare them with the other DISC styles. In your opinion, where do you feel major conflict would most likely occur?

    In the D/I combination -

    In the D/S combination -

    In the D/C combination -

2. In your opinion, which combinations have the greatest potential for misunderstanding? Which would have the least?

Understanding High D Representative Patterns

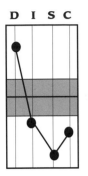

Primary D

Solomon, Rahab *

1- PRIMARY DRIVE:	Very independent in seeking solutions to problems	Ecc. 2:1-11
2- PERSONAL GIFTEDNESS:	Innovative problem solver; able to directly influence others' actions	I Kings 3:16-28 Joshua 2, 6
3- INSTINCTIVE FEARS:	Loss of control	I Kings 2:13-25
4- BLIND SPOT:	Seeing the need to be accountable to others	I Kings 11:1-13

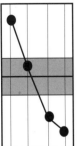

D/ I

Joshua, Sarah *

1- PRIMARY DRIVE:	Strength of character	Joshua 24:1-16, 31
2- PERSONAL GIFTEDNESS:	Takes charge; acts as catalyst to carry out difficult assignments	Joshua 1:1-18
3- INSTINCTIVE FEARS:	Slowness, especially in seeing a task or goal accomplished	Genesis 16:1-3
4- BLIND SPOTS:	Seeing where their actions contribute to negative consequences	Genesis 16:1-3

D equal I

Apollos, Stephen, and Lydia *

1- PRIMARY DRIVE:	Strong drive to control their environment by persuasion	Acts 18:24-28 Acts 16:13-15,40
2- PERSONAL GIFTEDNESS:	Gifted with verbal skills; can be intimidating	Acts 7:2-53 Acts 7:54:-60
3- INSTINCTIVE FEARS:	Not having authority to contol events; can misrepresent the facts	Genesis 29:15-25 Genesis 29:26-30
4- BLIND SPOTS:	Understanding their aggressive style can cause others to resort to covert action	Genesis 31:26-31 Acts 6:8-14

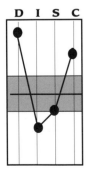

D/C

Paul, Rachel *, Michal *

1- PRIMARY DRIVE:	Being the front-runner in developing new concepts	Gal 1:15-16 Gal. 2:1-10
2- PERSONAL GIFTEDNESS:	Being the instrument in bringing about change to make old systems better	Gal. 2:15-16 Acts 15:1-29
3- INSTINCTIVE FEARS:	Others failing to measure up to their standards	Gal. 2:11-14
4-BLIND SPOTS:	Understanding that *grace* is a critical factor in implementing standards and principles	Acts 15:36-40

* Tendencies indicate a pattern, but not enough scriptural content to make a confident association.

High D Discovery Exercise

In your opinion, what tendencies make the High D unique?

How do the specific High D patterns differ from one another?

Pure D -

D/I -

D equal I -

D/C -

High D's fear being taken advantage of and have a tendency to react forcefully when their territory is threatened. Read I Kings 2:12-25. What did Adonijah, Solomon's older brother, ask of Bathsheba? What did Bathsheba do?

If Solomon had granted his brother's request, Adonijah could have laid claims to the throne. How did Solomon react to his mother's request? How did he respond to his brother? How does this apply to High D behavior?

A Look Ahead

In the next lesson, we will look at what causes High D's to react to stress the way they do. In addition, we will suggest ways you can help the High D. Finally, we will study how Jesus dealt with Paul to help him grow in obedience and maturity.

RESPONDING TO THE NEEDS OF THE DOMINANCE PERSONALITY

Assignment:
Understanding How Others Misunderstand You,
textbook chapter 6, pages 101-124

If you are to understand how to love a High D, you must first recognize what happens to him when certain of his needs are not met. As with other profiles, a High D will protect himself in a predictable way. The High D needs an environment that offers difficult assignments along with authority to confront the challenges of the task. When High D profiles sense outside pressures preventing him from achieving his personal goals, boiling internal energy begins to mount. Frequently, he releases this energy in an explosion of anger and/or punitive action directed toward those blocking his goals.

In this session, we will describe the situations that typically cause the High D to explode. In addition, we will look at a biblical case study in which a High D finds himself in a typical stress situation resulting in negative consequences.

Also, we will look at what elements are necessary to give the High D the best opportunity to grow in stressful situations. We will review a biblical case study showing how Jesus created a specific environment for the Apostle Paul so that he had the opportunity to minister under God's authority and not his own. You will be given the opportunity to test the concepts discussed in this session through a series of questions designed for small group discussion.

Understanding High D Stress

Need Issues: • Being in *control*
                     • Accomplishing
                         personal goals

The High D begins to encounter stress when:

1. He has to submit to *authority* and *lose control*
2. He has his personal goal *blocked* or *threatened*
3. His common reaction is to *actively confront the person(s) creating the threat*
4. Their normal response will be to *confront* back
5. That results in *all-out confrontation---jungle warfare*
6. Commuinications deteriorates to a *messenger system*

Biblical Case Study : Exodus 5:1 - 6:11

Read the Scripture passage. What were the instructions Moses and Aaron communicated to Pharaoh, the High D? If God's plan were implemented, what effect would that have on Pharaoh's construction program---building monuments with his name on them? What was his response and what actions did he take to counter their plan? What was the response of Israel to Moses and Aaron? What did Moses and Aaron do? What was God's response? What D tendencies are present?

Understanding the High D Environment

HOW TO RESPOND TO A HIGH D
- Be firm and direct
- Focus on actions and goals
- Confrontation may be necessary to get his or her attention

HOW TO RELATE TO A HIGH D
- Be brief and to the point and leave
- Explain "how to achieve goals" using logic with an action plan
- Don't expect agreement; allow time to consider your ideas

HOW TO REINFORCE THE HIGH D
- Repeat the plan of action focusing on goals, objective, and results
- Give bottom-line instructions
- Get out of the way

Assignment

If you know a High D, have him review the list above. Have the D pick a least one element that is important and meaningful in creating a loving environment for him. Record his response below.

Optional exercise

To me, the most interesting element of the High D environment is:

Understanding Christ's style of loving Paul

Read Acts 9:1-22. In the left column are the critical verses of the passage which describe Christ's actions and Paul's reactions. In the right column, describe in your own words the environment that Jesus created as He spoke to Paul. How does it compare to the suggestions listed on the previous page in loving the High D profiles?

Christ's actions and Paul's reactions	Your insights into Jesus' environment
"And it came about that as he journeyed, he was approaching Damascus, and suddenly a light from heaven flashed around him; and he fell to the ground, and heard a voice saying to him, 'Saul, Saul, why are you persecuting Me?'	Describe Jesus' tone as He responded to Paul?
And he said, 'Who art Thou, Lord?' and He said, 'I am Jesus whom you are persecuting, but rise, and enter the city, and it shall be told you what you must do....' And Saul got up from the ground, and though his eyes were open, he could see nothing; and leading him by the hand, they brought him into Damascus. And he was three days without sight, and neither ate nor drank....	What was the length of Jesus' message to Paul and what were the instructions?
And Ananias departed and entered the house, and after laying his hands on him said, 'Brother Saul, the Lord Jesus, who appeared to you on the road by which you were coming, has sent me so that you may regain your sight, and be filled with the Holy Spirit.' And immediately there fell from his eyes something like scales, and he regained his sight, and he arose and was baptized; and he took food and was strengthened. Now for several days he was with the disciples who were at Damascus, and immediately he began to proclaim Jesus in the synagogues, saying, 'He is the Son of God.'"	How did Ananias reinforce Jesus' message and what was Paul's response?

DISCovering the High D:
Worksheet for High D Profiles

This worksheet and the worksheet that immediately follows go together and should be discussed by specific groups. High D profiles should use this worksheet; Low D profiles (I's, S's, and C's) should use the worksheet on the next page.

After all questions have been answered, share your answers with your partner, discussing your responses to questions 1a,b, and c, then question 2, and so on. If you are using a discussion group method, select a spokesman to share the consensus of the group's findings. Then join the other three profiles for the group discussion.

1a.   If I had to describe my behavior in three phrases, I would choose the following words...

1b.   I like jobs that have tasks which involve...

1c.   But I would rather delegate tasks that are involved with...

2.   If I had to select three components from the list on page 48 to better respond, relate, and reinforce me, they would be...

3.   As I reflect on how Jesus responded to Paul in Acts 9, He would also have ministered to me when He...

4a.   When I am under stress, the most loving thing you can do for me is...

4b.   I best deal with personal anger by...

5.   In order to develop better relationships with the other profiles, I continually need to work on the following areas of my behavioral style:

        in relating to the High I

        in relating to the High S

        in relating to the High C

Loving the High D:
<u>Worksheet for Low D profiles</u>

This worksheet is to be filled out by the Low D profiles (I's, S's, and C's) at the same time the High D's are filling out their worksheet. After you have answered all of the questions, share your answers. If you are using a discussion group method, divide into at least three groups (High I's, High S's, and High C's) and select a spokesman for each group. Rejoin the High D's and share the consensus of the group's findings discussing one question at a time, alternating between the High D worksheet and the Low D worksheet.

1.   Areas of my life where I need the gifts of the High D:

2.   As I reflect on the ways to respond, relate and reinforce the High D listed on page 48, the most difficult component for me to create and communicate is:

3.   The one component Jesus used in Acts 9 in communicating with Paul that I need to work on in relating to the High D is:

4.   As I review my differences in styles with the High D, I see my greatest potential for conflict to be:

        because

5.   In order to build a better personal and working relationship with High "D's", I need to be willing to modify my need to/for:

        Bonus Question:

6.   If I were planning a date or function with a High D, I would include the following activities:

UNDERSTANDING THE INFLUENCING STYLE

Assignment:
Understanding How Others Misunderstand You,
textbook chapter 7, pages 125-142

The **Influencing** or **High I** individual is outgoing, persuasive, gregarious, and optimistic. He can usually see some good in any situation. He is principally interested in people, their problems, and their activities. High I's meet people easily and can be on a first-name basis with someone the first time they meet him or her.

In this session we will focus on how the Influencing styles work and relate to the other profiles. We will discuss how the High I's are likely to be misunderstood by others. The goal of this session is to gain awareness of why conflicts occur with the Influencing profiles and what can be done to build growing and solid relationships.

In this session, we will also discuss the basic tendencies of the High I and the family of Influencing profile patterns: **Pure I, I/D, I/S, I/C.** We will also discuss the biblical characters that represent the four High I groups.

Understanding High I Tendencies and Skills

Basic Tendencies

1. High I's have a tendency *to be optimistic* and have a natural gift for *trusting* and *believing* in others by projecting unconditional acceptance.

2. High I's tend to be *socially oriented* and are the most comfortable when they are relating to and interacting with people. They have the gift of reaching out to strangers.

3. High I's are motivated by *social recognition.*

4. The basic fear of the High I is *social rejection.*

5. The basic blind spot for the High I is *being objective* when social pressure is present.

Basic Strengths

The High I's have excellent social skills, but when a High I's tendencies are out of control, he is likely to compromise or overlook critical commitments. To counterbalance those traits, the High I needs to have individuals around him who have strenths that are complementary to his. Below are examples of various High I strengths and corresponding complementary strengths of other profiles. In the last column the final three complementary profiles have been left out. Which patterns best represent the complementary strength?

Strength of the High I Profile	Complementary Strengths needed	Patterns who have the complementary strength
Emotionally responsive	Objective problem solver	D
Optimistic starter	Follow-through	S
Confident	Realistic	C
Socially sensitive	Making unpopular decisions	D
Verbally enthusiastic	Good listener	S
Trusting and affirming	Asking critical questions	C

53

Understanding How the High I Relates to Others

The following compatibility chart identifies the natural manner in which an Influencing person generally relates to each DISC behavioral style in social relationships and in job tasks.

Profile Teams	Excellent Chemistry			Requires Effort				Constant Work		
	10	9	8	7	6	5	4	3	2	1
I - I	R									T
I - D			R					T		
I - S		T				R				
I - C					T	R				

KEY

R = Social Relationships
T = Job Tasks

10 = Best Possible
1 = Poorest Possible

Definitions

I - I Team: High I's relate well to each other because they enjoy socializing and having fun together. However, their work ethic is poor because they enjoy talking so much that they seldom have time for work.

I - D Team: Because both High I's and D's enjoy environments which include variety and change, the generally maintain good social relationships. However, when they begin to work together, they differences in focus can be come a problem. High I's have a tendency to make decisions based on relationships, whereas High D's do so based on cold facts and the bottom line.

I - S Team: High I's work well with High S's because the I's have the verbal skills to sell the team's ideas, whereas the S's will commit to making sure the work is completed.   Their personal relationship often suffers because High I's have a tendency to be inconsistent with their commitments, and are constantly changing their plans, whereas the High S's desire is for stability and loyalty.

I - C Team: The work relationship between I and C is generally good because the I's need and depend on the C's ability to research the facts. Like the High S, the C's generally admire the I's ability to sell their ideas. Their personal relationship often suffers because the I's are free-spirited and impulsive, whereas the C's desire structure with no surprises.

Misunderstanding the HIGH I

Study the characteristics below and circle the traits that, in your opinion, could tend to lead to misunderstandings.

Characteristics of the High I

1. Influencing Tendencies include:
   contacting people,
   generating enthusiasm,
   making a flavorable impression.

2. Desires an environment with :
   democratic relationship,
   group activities outside of the job,
   freedom from control and details.

3. Under pressure:
   Becomes soft and persuadable,
   emotional, verbal, and assertive,
   can become manipulative.

Characteristics of the other DISC styles

Tendencies of other DISC styles:
High D styles - getting results
High S styles - calming excited people
High C styles - critical of performance

Desires an environment with:
High D styles - personal control
High S styles - minimal infringement on home
High C styles - standard operating procedures

Under pressure:
High D styles - confrontative and aggressive
High S styles - becomes quiet and withdrawn
High C styles - becomes restrained and
                    sensitive to criticism

Exploring exercise :

1. Study each of the three High I characteristics and compare them with the other DISC styles. In your opinion, where do you feel major conflict would most likely occur?

    In the I/D combination -

    In the I/S combination -

    In the I/C combination -

2. In your opinion, which combinations have the greatest potential for misunderstanding? Which would have the least?

Understanding High I Representative Patterns

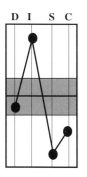

Primary I — King Saul, Aaron

1- PRIMARY DRIVE:	Creation of a favorable, friendly environment	I Samuel 15:6-13
2- PERSONAL GIFTEDNESS:	Quick of tongue; special ability to affirm and encourage others	Exodus 4:28-31 I Samuel 15:15
3- INSTINCTIVE FEARS:	Having to face social rejection	I Samuel 15:19-27
4- BLIND SPOT:	Connecting commitments to action when encountering social pressure	I Samuel 15:1-3 Exodus 24, 32:1-6

I/ D — Peter, Rebekah *

1- PRIMARY DRIVE:	Reaching out to strangers, sincere desire to help people	Genesis 24:53-58 Acts 3:1-6
2- PERSONAL GIFTEDNESS:	Influencing others with verbal persuasion; poised speaker	Acts 3:12-26,4:4 Acts 4:7-12
3- INSTINCTIVE FEARS:	Being rejected by friends	Galatians 2:11-12
4- BLIND SPOTS:	Remembering past commitments in an unfavorable environment	Matthew 26:31-35 Luke 22:54-62

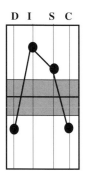

I/S — Barnabas, Abigail

1- PRIMARY DRIVE:	Projecting encouragement; maintaining peace and harmony	Acts 4:36-37 I Samuel 25:13-35
2- PERSONAL GIFTEDNESS:	Sees the potential in people in spite of their flaws	Acts 9:26-27 Acts 15:36-39
3- INSTINCTIVE FEARS:	Disappointing friends; having to continually experience disharmony	Galatians 2:13 Acts 15:38-39
4- BLIND SPOTS:	Knowing when an abusive situation is critical enough to confront	I Samuel 25:2-3,19, 36

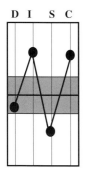

I/C — David, Mary Magdalene*, Miriam*

1- PRIMARY DRIVE:	Being innovative with flair	I Samuel 17:26-54
2- PERSONAL GIFTEDNESS:	Working through people and having fun	I Samuel 18:20-30
3- INSTINCTIVE FEARS:	Coming under public criticism; made to look bad before peers	I Kings 2:8-9
4- BLIND SPOTS:	Being rational when under emotional pressure	II Samuel 11:1-27 Psalm 32

* Tendencies indicate a pattern, but not enough scriptural content to make a confident association.

High I Discovery Exercise

In your opinion, what tendencies make the High I different from the High D?

What are some observable differences in the High I Representative Patterns?

Pure I

I/D

I/S

I/C

High I's fear loss of *social recognition.* If they have to make a choice between maintaining a principle or a relationship, they will generally sacrifice their commitment to the principle.

Read I Samuel 15:1-31. What was Saul's assignment? What principles did he compromise? When Samuel confronted him, what reasons did he give?

In verse 30, what specific issue concerned him? How does this apply to the High I?

A Look Ahead

In the next lesson, we will look at what causes High I's to react to stress as they do. In addidtion, we will suggest ways you can help the High I's. Finally, we will study how Jesus dealt with Peter in order to help him become the type of leader He needed.

RESPONDING TO THE NEEDS OF THE INFLUENCING PERSONALITY

Assignment:
Understanding How Others Miunderstand You,
textbook chapter 8, pages 143-163

If you are to understand how to love a High I, you must first be aware of what typically happens to a High I when certain of his needs are not met. High I's want to be surrounded by people who come together in a positive, friendly environment. High I's enjoy situations that allow verbal interaction along with stimulating and fun activities. High I's fear social rejection. When that type of pressure presents itself, the High I will frequently bend with the pressure in order to maintain relationships. Whereas the High D will be concerned with accomplishing a set of goals, the High I will focus on reaching out to people.

In this session we will look at the situations that commonly cause the High I to cave in to pressure. We will study a biblical case study that shows a High I in a typical series of stressful events that resulted in a nongrowth experience for all those involved in the situation.

We will also look at the elements that are necessary to give the High I the best opportunity to grow. In addition, we will review a biblical case study in which Jesus created a specific environment for Peter so that he had the opportunity to work through his negative traits and mature. You will have the chance to interact with a series of questions focusing on the needs of the High I. The purpose of this exercise is to build an awareness of who the High I is and how you can be more effective in loving him.

Understanding High I Stress

Need Issues: • Maintaining a positive, social relationship with peers

The High I begins to encounter stress when:

1. Clear and very *detailed* instructions are given by a superior requiring a *specific action plan*
2. Appearing to listen, the High I gives hearty *agreement* and *commitment* to the superior's plan and instructions
3. Later, the High I's *peers* present a different set of ideas that are in total disagreement with the superior's plan and instructions
4. Rather than communicate previous commitments, the I *caves in to social pressure* and takes action on the peers' desires
5. The superior returns and then confronts the I on the reasons for the change
6. Using his verbal skills, the I responds by *shifting blame to others*

Biblical Case Study:
Exodus 20:2-4; 24:3, 8, 12-14; 32:1-6, 21-24

Read the Scripture passages. How would you interpret the first two commandments God gave Moses? What was the response of the nation of Israel to those commandments? What was Aaron's responsibility?

Later, in Exodus 32, what did the people ask Aaron to do? What could he have done? When Moses confronted Aaron concerning his action, how did Aaron respond? What I tendencies are apparent?

59

Understanding the High I Environment

- **HOW TO RESPOND TO A HIGH I**
  Be friendly and positive
  Allow for informal dialogue
  Allow time for stimulating and fun activities before getting to business

- **HOW TO RELATE TO A HIGH I**
  Use friendly voice tones
  Allow him or her time to verbalize his or her feelings
  You transfer talk to an action plan

- **HOW TO REINFORCE THE HIGH I**
  Offer encouragement and incentives for taking on tasks.
  You organize the action plan
  Communicate positive social recognition in front of peers

Aaron

Assignment

If you know a High I, have him review the list above. Have him pick a least one element that is important and meaningful in creating a loving environment for him. Record his response below.

Optional exercise

To me, the most interesting element of the High I environment is:

60

Understanding Jesus' style of loving Peter

Read John 21:1-22. In the left column, are the critical verses of the passage which describe Jesus' actions and Peter's reactions. In the right column, describe in your own words the environment that Jesus created as He spoke to Peter. How does it compare to the suggestions listed on the previous page in loving the High I profiles?

Jesus' actions and Peter's reactions	Your insights into Jesus' environment
"Simon Peter said the them, 'I am going fishing.' They said to him, 'We will also come with you.' They went out,...and that night they caught nothing.... Jesus stood on the beach...and said to them,' Children, you do not have any fish, do you?' They answered Him,'No.' And He said to them, 'Cast the net on the right-hand side of the boat, and you will find a catch.' They cast...and were not able to haul it in.... And so when they got out upon the land, they saw a charcoal fire already laid, and fish placed on it, and bread. Jesus said to them, 'Come and have breakfast'....and [He] took the bread, and gave them, and the fish likewise."...	What was the tone set by Jesus': friendly or confrontational?
So when they finished breakfast, Jesus [asked] Peter,'Simon, do you love Me?'He said to Him, 'Yes Lord; You know that I love You.' He said to him,'Tend My lambs.' He said... a second time,'Simon,...do you love Me?' He said to Him, 'Yes Lord; You know that I love You.' He said to him, 'Shepherd My sheep.' He said to him the third time,'Simon, do you love Me?' Peter was grieved ....And said to Him,'Lord, You know all things; You know that I love You.' Jesus said to him, 'Tend My sheep....	What was the point of Jesus' questions to Peter? What did it cause Peter to do? What was Jesus' response and was it an action plan?
When you grow old, you will stretch out your hands, and someone else will gird you , and bring you where you do not wish to go. Now this He said, signifying by what kind of death he would glorify God. And... He said to him,' Follow Me!'"	Jesus restored Peter to a place of authority among the Apostles. Who was listening to this affirmation message? What impact do you think it made on Peter?

DISCovering the High I:
Worksheet for High I Profiles

       This worksheet and the worksheet that immediately follows go together and should be discussed by specific groups. High I profiles should use this worksheet; Low I profiles (D's, S's, and C's) should use the worksheet on the next page.
       After all questions have been answered, share your answers with your partner, discussing your responses to question 1, then question 2, and so on. If you are using a discussion group method, select a spokesman to share the consensus of the group's findings. Then join the other three profiles for the group discussion.

1a.   If I had to describe my behavior in three phrases, I would choose the following words...

1b.   I like jobs that have tasks which involve...

1c.   But I would rather delegate tasks that are involved with...

2.   If I had to select three components from the list on page 60 to better respond, relate and reinforce me, they would be...

3.   As I reflect on how Jesus responded to Peter in John 21, He would also have ministered to me when He...

4a.   When I am under stress, the most loving thing you can do for me is...

4b.   I have learned not to be influenced by social pressure by...

5.   In order to develop better relationships with the other profiles, I continually need to work on the following areas of my behavioral style:

in relating to the High D

in relating to the High S

in relating to the High C

Loving the High I:
Worksheet for Low I profiles

       This worksheet is to be filled out by the Low I profiles (D's, S's, and C's) at the same time the High I's are filling out their worksheet. After you have answered all of the questions, share your answers. If you are using a discussion group method, divide into at least three groups (High D's, High S's, and High C's) and select a spokesman for each group. Rejoin the High I's and share the consensus of the group's findings discussing one question at a time, alternating between the High D worksheet and the Low I worksheet.

1.   Areas of my life where I need the gifts of the High I:

2.   As I reflect on the ways to respond, relate, and reinforce the High I listed on page 60, the most difficult component for me to create and communicate is:

3.   The one component Jesus used in John 21 in communicating with Peter that I need to work on in relating to the High I is:

4.   As I review my differences in styles with the High I, I see my greatest potential for conflict to be:

       because

5.   In order to build a better personal and working relationship with High I's, I need to be willing to modify my need to/for:

       Bonus Question:

6.   If I were planning a date or function with a High I , I would include the following activities:

UNDERSTANDING THE STEADINESS STYLE

Assignment:
Understanding How Others Misunderstand You,
textbook chapter 9, pages 165-183

The **Steadiness** or **High S** individual is characterized by a more laid-back approach to life. High S's tend to be more introverted and generally possess good listening skills. High S's generally remain calm during stressful situations and patiently go about their work in an orderly manner. Whereas High I's desire public recognition, High S's prefer to stay behind the scenes. Whereas High D's operate well in an unfavorable environment, High S's prefer a predictable, stable climate.

In this session we will focus on how the Steadiness profile tends to be misunderstood by those who are different from them. Our goal is to understand why High S's respond the way they do and to gain insights into how to support them.

In this session, we will also discuss the basic tendencies of the High S family of Steadiness profile patterns: **Pure S, S/D, S/I, and S/C/D.** We will also discuss the biblical characters that represent the four High S groups.

Understanding High S Tendencies and Skills

Basic Tendencies

1. High S's take a *pragmatic* approach to problem solving and prefer to be *team* players.

2. High S's put a high value on the *stablility* of the home.

3. High S's are motivated by *traditional* procedures.

4. The basic fears of High S's are *disharmony* and *instability*.

5. The basic blind spot for High S's is not knowing when to *challenge the status quo*.

Basic Strengths

The High S's have many unique skills, but if these strengths are unchecked, imbalance can occur. To counterbalance the High S's skills, a complementary DIC skill is needed. Below are examples of various High S strengths and corresponding supportive strengths of other profiles. In the last column the final three complementary profiles have been left out. Which patterns best represent the complementary strength?

Strength of the High S profile	Complementary strengths needed	Patterns who have the complementary strength
Accommodating	Challenging	D
Patient	Spontaneous	I
Amiable	Asking critical questions	C
Calm	Aggressive	D
Good listener	Expressive	I
Easy going	Concerned about details	C

Understanding How the High S Relates to Others

The following compatibility chart identifies the natural manner in which a Steadiness person generally relates to each DISC behavioral style in social relationships and in job tasks.

Profile Teams	Excellent Chemistry			Requires Effort				Constant Work		
	10	9	8	7	6	5	4	3	2	1
S - D	T							R		
S - I	T					R				
S - S	R		T							
S - C		R	T							

KEY

R = Social Relationships
T = Job Tasks

10 = Best Possible
1 = Poorest Possible

Definitions

S - D Team: High D's have good start-up skills and High S's have good follow-up skills. Personal relationships tend to be fair due to the fact that High S individuals desire reassurances and prefer close relationships, whereas High D individuals tend to be more independent, resist closeness, and frequently create disharmony.

S - I Team: High I's are spontaneous and desire harmony but have difficulty maintaining their focus. They also often lack follow-through. The relationship between the High I and the High S frequently becomes strained because the High S desires stability and status quo, whereas the High I needs spontaneity and change.

S - S Team: High S's get along with other High S's because they both respond to stability and family values. They can work well if they can overcome a tendency toward putting off responsibilities.

S - C Team: The High C will generally be more concerned about the task at hand, whereas the High S will be concerned with getting along with others. Those two approaches are generally congruent skills in work situations. High S's and High C's generally relate well to each other because both are committed to maintaining harmony and the status quo.

Misunderstanding the HIGH S

Study the characteristics below and circle the traits that, in your opinion, could tend to lead to misunderstandings.

Characteristics of the High S

1. Steadiness Tendencies include:
   sitting or staying in one place,
   one task at a time,
   a predictable work pattern.

2. Desires an environment with :
   status quo unless given reasons for change,
   traditional procedures,
   time to adjust to change.

3. Management style:
   desires feedback from others,
   allows others freedom to operate,
   establishes and follows procedures.

Characteristics of the other DISC styles

Tendencies of other DISC styles:
High D styles - want to create change often
High I styles - desire varied activities
High C styles - like things in their right place

Desires an environment with:
High D styles - challenging and varying activities
High I styles - unstructured activities
High C styles - no sudden or abrupt changes

Management style:
High D styles - autocratic and authoritative
High I styles - democratic and informal
High C styles - bureaucratic; going by the book

Exploring exercise :

1. Study each of the three High S characteristics and compare them with the other DISC styles. In your opinion, where do you feel major conflict would most likely occur?

   In the S/D combination -

   In the S/I combination -

   In the S/C combination -

2. In your opinion, which combinations have the greatest potential for misunderstanding? Which would have the least?

Understanding High S Representative Patterns

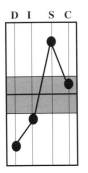

Primary S   **Isaac, Dorcas ***

1- PRIMARY DRIVE:	Controlled, secure environment	Genesis 24:63-67
2- PERSONAL GIFTEDNESS:	Honoring those in authority	Genesis 22:1-9
	Maintaining traditions	Genesis 28:1-5
3- INSTINCTIVE FEARS:	Being strong; confronting others	Genesis 26:7-23
4- BLIND SPOT:	Being confident in knowing their pattern has strengths	Genesis 26:26-33

S/ D   **Nehemiah, Joseph, Martha ***

1- PRIMARY DRIVE:	Diligence in taking ownership of tasks; industrious	Nehemiah 2:5-10
2- PERSONAL GIFTEDNESS:	Follow-through in completing task, administrative duties	Nehemiah 6:15 Genesis 39:1-6
3- INSTINCTIVE FEARS:	Non compliance to standards	Nehemiah 13:10-25
4- BLIND SPOTS:	Awareness that relationships are as important as completing tasks	Luke 10:38-42 John 11:20-28

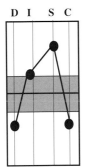

S/I   **Abraham, Hannah ***

1- PRIMARY DRIVE:	Security of family, maintaining peace and harmony	Genesis 14 Genesis 18:22-33
2- PERSONAL GIFTEDNESS:	Showing hospitality, being loyal to friends, expressing kindness	Genesis 18:1-8 I Samuel 1:17-38, 2:11
3- INSTINCTIVE FEARS:	Dissension and conflict	Genesis 13:7-9
4- BLIND SPOTS:	Being able to free oneself of security blankets	Acts 7:2-3, Genesis 11:31; 12:1-5

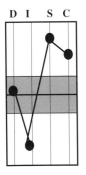

S/C/D   **Jacob, James (Acts 15) Anna ***

1- PRIMARY DRIVE:	Determination and tenacity	Genesis 32:24-30
2- PERSONAL GIFTEDNESS:	Steadily working through complex problems	Genesis 30:25-43
3- INSTINCTIVE FEARS:	Having to publicly match wits with strong personalities in selling ideas	Genesis 31:1-7, 26-31
4- BLIND SPOTS:	Being preoccupied with worry	Genesis 33:1-4

* Tendencies indicate a pattern, but not enough scriptural content to make a confident association.

High S Discovery Exercise

In your opinion, how is the High S different from the High D and the High I?

What are some observable differences in the High S Representative Patterns?

Pure S

S/D

S/I

S/C/D

High S's are uncomfortable with *change* and fear *dissension* and *conflict*. A predictable response for High S profiles is to avoid confrontation if possible.

Read Genesis 26:1-22. Describe how Isaac handled potential conflict. How does his behavior demonstrate High S tendencies?

A Look Ahead

In the next lesson, we will look at what causes High S's to react to stress in the way that they do. In addition, we will look at what you can do to help them. Finally, we will study how the Lord supported Abraham.

RESPONDING TO THE NEEDS OF THE STEADINESS PERSONALITY

Assignment:

Understanding How Others Misunderstand You,
textbook chapter 10, pages 185-203

To understand how to love the High S, you must first understand what happens to a High S when certain of his needs are not met. As with other profiles , High S's will protect themselves, and their reactions are predictable. Specifically, the High S needs a stable environment free of conflict. When the opposite condition is present High S profiles become uncomfortable, internalize the pressure, and begin to withdraw. Whereas the High D becomes aggressive when he is under pressure, the High S will flee and go into a shell. Whereas the High I becomes emotional and talkative under pressure, the High S becomes unemotional and quiet.

In this session we will describe situations that commonly cause the High S profile to react in the way we outlined above. In addition, we will look at a biblical case study that amplifies what typically happens.

We will also look at the elements that are necessary to give the High S the best opportunity to grow through stressful situations. In addition, you will be asked to review a biblical case study in which God provides Abraham with the positive elements he needs to naturally grow in his trust in the Lord. Finally, you will be given the opportunity to test the concepts presented in this session through responding to a series of questions designed for small group discussion.

Understanding High S Stress

Need Issues:
- An environment free of conflict (particularly within the home)
- Time to adjust to change

The High S begins to encounter stress when his:

1. Routine action does not create the expected *results*
2. The S's partner then implements an aggressive "take control" strategy
3. The S typically complies, but produces *passive results*
4. The S's partner then uses stronger *confrontive measures*, thinking that *more pressure* is an even better strategy
5. This results in the S's adopting a passive-aggressive response, i.e., *noninvolvement*, *silence*, or the *turtle syndrome*

Biblical Case Study: Genesis 15:1-5; 16:1-6

Read the Scripture passages and determine the promise God gave Abraham. Describe Sarah's response to God's plan when she spoke to Abraham in Genesis 16. Describe Abraham's reaction. (Remember, Sarah is a D, and Abraham is an S.)

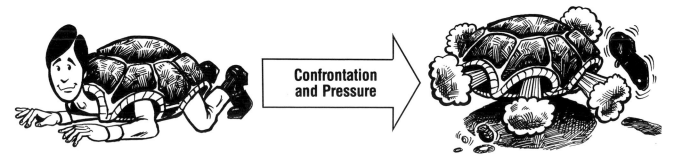

Confrontation and Pressure

Understanding the High S Environment

HOW TO RESPOND TO A HIGH S
- Be nonthreatening and patient
- Allow time to process and adjust to change
- Make allowances for family

HOW TO RELATE TO A HIGH S
- Use friendly tones when instructing
- Give personal, nonverbal assurances
- Allow time to process information

HOW TO REINFORCE THE HIGH S
- Patiently repeat instructions
- Provide hands-on reinforcement
- Be patient in allowing time to take ownership

me Peggy Russell

Assignment

If you know a High S, have him review the list above. Have him pick a least one element that is important and meaningful in creating a loving environment for him. Record his response below.

Optional Exercise

To me, the most interesting element of the High S environment is:

"Isn't there an easier way?!!"

72

Understanding God's style of loving Abraham

Read Acts 7:2-5; Joshua 24:2-3; Genesis 11:31-32;12:1-7; 13:1-18. In the left column, are the critical verses of the passage which describe God's actions and Abraham's reactions. In the right column, describe in your own words the environment that God created as He spoke to Abraham. How does it compare to the suggestions listed on the previous page in loving the High S profiles?

God's actions and Abraham's reactions	Your insights to God's environment
"God appeared...to Abraham when he was in Ur, before he lived in Haran, And said to Him, 'DEPART FROM YOUR COUNTRY AND <u>YOUR RELATIVES,</u> AND COME INTO THE LAND THAT I WILL SHOW YOU.' And Terah took Abram his son, and Lot [Abraham's nephew] ...and Sarai, Abram's wife; and they went out together from Ur...in order to enter the land of Canaan; and they went as far as Haran, and settled there...And Terah died in Haran.	What did God ask of Abraham ? How clear were His instructions on the subject of Abraham leaving his family? How did Abraham do?
Now the Lord said to Abram, 'God forth from your country, And from <u>your relatives</u> And from <u>your father's house,</u> To the land I will show you; And I will make you a great nation, And I will bless you, And make your name great; And so you shall be a blessing....' So Abraham went forth as the Lord had spoken to him; and Lot went with him. [*And there was strife between the herdsmen of Lot and Abraham and they separated.*]	What was God's tone and message the second time they talked. Was the message regarding the family clear? What did Abraham do?
And the Lord said to Abram, after Lot had separated from him, 'Now lift up your eyes and look from this place where you are...for all the land which you see, I will give it to you and to your descendants forever.... Arise, walk about the land through its length and breadth; for I will give it to you.'" [*And Abraham settled in the land.*]	What was God's tone and message the third time they talked? What did Abraham do?

DISCovering the High S:
Worksheet for High S Profiles

This worksheet and the worksheet that immediately follows go together and should be discussed by specific groups. High S profiles should use this worksheet; Low S profiles (D's, I's, and C's) should use the worksheet on the next page.

After all questions have been answered, share your answers with your partner, discussing your responses to question 1, then question 2, and so on. If you are using a discussion group method, select a spokesman to share the consensus of the group's findings. Then join the other three profiles for the group discussion.

1a.   If I had to describe my behavior in three phrases, I would choose the following words...

1b.   I like jobs that have tasks which involve...

1c.   But I would rather delegate tasks that are involved with...

2.   If I had to select three components from the list on page 72 to better respond, relate, and reinforce me, they would be...

3.   As I reflect on how God responded to Abraham, He would also have ministered to me when He...

4a.   When I am under stress, the most loving thing you can do for me is

4b.   I have learned to overcome my need for the status quo by

5.   In order to develop better relationships with the other profiles, I continually need to work on the following areas of my behavioral style:

        in relating to the High D

        in relating to the High I

        in relating to the High C

Loving the High S:
Worksheet for Low S profiles

This worksheet is to be filled out by the Low S profiles (D's, I's, and C's) at the same time the High S's are filling out their worksheet. After you have answered all of the questions, share your answers. If you are using a discussion group method, divide into at least three groups (High D's, High I's, and High C's) and select a spokesman for each group. Rejoin the high S's and share the consensus of the groups's findings, discussing one question at a time, alternating between the High S worksheet and the Low S worksheet.

1.　　Areas of my life where I need the gifts of the High S:

2.　　As I reflect on the ways to respond, relate, and reinforce the High S listed on page 72, the most difficult component for me to create and communicate is:

3.　　The one component God used in communicating with Abraham that I need to work on in relating to a High S is :

4.　　As I review my differences in styles with the High S, I see my greatest potential for conflict to be:

　　　because

5.　　In order to build a better personal and working relationship with High S's, I need to be willing to modify my need to/for:

　　　Bonus Question:

6.　　If I were planning a date or function with a High S , I would include the following activities:

UNDERSTANDING THE COMPLIANCE STYLE

Assignment:
Understanding How Others Misunderstand You,
textbook chapter 11, pages 205-226

Compliance, or **High C**, individuals have concerns for details and quality control. They tend to be critical thinkers and check for accuracy. Whereas High I's tend to be extremely forgiving of personal errors, High C's have a tendency to remember their mistakes and be self-critical. Whereas the High D's will behave aggressively in an unfavorable environment, High C's will respond more cautiously. Whereas the High S's will initially focus on the relational issues, High C's will focus on tasks.

In this lesson we will focus on how the Compliance style relates to the other profiles. We will also study how the High C tends to be misunderstood. Our goal will be to understand why conflicts occur with the Compliance profiles and what can be done to help them work through sensitive issues in their lives. If this can be done, the High C's will be freed to mature in their walk with the Lord.

In addition, we will discuss the basic tendencies of the High C and the family of Compliant Profile Patterns: **Pure C, C/S/D, C/I/S, and C/S**. Positive biblical characters will be associated with each of the four High C groups.

Understanding High C Tendencies and Skills

Basic Tendencies

1. High C's have the tendency to be concerned with accuracy and precision.

2. Before assuming a new task, a High C will have a tendency to ask many clarification questions.

3. When assuming a new task, a High C will remain cautious. He is motivated by the "proper way" of doing things.

4. The basic fear of the High C is that someone will criticize his work.

5. The basic blind spot for High C is continually having to battle unrealistic expection of themselves and others.

Basic Strengths

The High C's has special quality-control skills, but if these are unchecked, imbalance can occur. To counterbalance the High C's skills, a complementary DIS skill is needed. Below are examples of various High C strengths and corresponding supportive strengths of other profiles. In the last column three complementary profiles have been left out. Which patterns best represent the complementary strength?

Strength of the High C profile	Complementary strengths needed	Patterns who have the complementary strength
Cautious	Decisive	D
Precise	Flexible	I
Thorough	Accommodating	S
Systematic thinker	Problem solver	
Well-prepared	Verbalizes thoughts of others	
Perfectionist	Practical	

Understanding How the High C Relates to Others

The following compatibility chart identifies the natural manner in which a Compliance person generally relates to each DISC behavioral style in social relationships and in job tasks.

Profile Teams	Excellent Chemistry			Requires Effort				Constant Work		
	10	9	8	7	6	5	4	3	2	1
C - D							T			R
C - I					T			R		
C - S		R	T							
C - C		R	T							

KEY

R = Social Relationships
T = Job Tasks

10 = Best Possible
1 = Poorest Possible

Definitions

C-D Team: The C's and D's have the most potential difficulty in working and relating together because of differences in expectations. The C's generally expect standards and rules to be followed, whereas the D's have a "the end justifies the means" outlook. Both need each other and, if they can resolve their expectation differences, they can become an effective team.

C-I Team: The work relationship between C and I is generally good because the C's generally lack the interpersonal skills of the High I. In contrast, the I's need the quality control skills of the C's to keep them out of trouble. Like the D/C combination, their personal relationship often suffers because of their differences in expectations. However, the issues are different. The C's hear the I's make verbal commitments and expect them to follow through; however, the I's intent is just to verbalize their thoughts.

C-S Team: The C's and S's relate and work well together because both are committed to maintain the environment and keeping the status quo. The C's offer the quality control, whereas the S's see to it that the work gets done in a timely manner.

C-C Team: The C's relate well to other C's because both share similar levels of sensitivity and concerns. Their work relationship is "good" but may have difficulties in completing projects on time because of their concern for "perfection." If production schedules are critical, it's best to team them with High S profiles.

Misunderstanding the HIGH C

Study the characteristics below and circle the traits that, in your opinion, could tend to lead to misunderstandings.

Characteristics of the High C

1. Compliance tendencies include:
   complying with authority,
   concentrating on key details,
   working under known
   circumstances.

2. Desires an environment with :
   security assurance,
   reassurances,
   no sudden or abrupt changes.

3. Response to stress:
   internalizes anger,
   desires to be alone, withdraws
   becomes worrisome; and
   becomes depressed.

Characteristics of the other DISC styles

Tendencies of other DISC styles:
High D styles - taking authority
High I styles - desire to help others
High S styles - demonstrating patience

Desires an environment with:
High D styles - "living on the edge"
High I styles - favorable working conditions
High S styles - traditional procedures

Response to stress:
High D styles - explosive anger
High I styles - wants to talk about it
High S styles - retreats into a shell, takes a nap

Exploring exercise :

1. Study each of the three High C characteristics and compare them with the other DISC styles. In your opinion, where do you feel major conflict would most likely occur?

   In the C/D combination -

   In the C/I combination -

   In the C/S combination -

2. In your opinion, which combinations have the greatest potential for misunderstanding? Which would have the least?

Understanding High C Representative Patterns

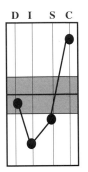

Primary C   **Luke, Esther •**

1- PRIMARY DRIVE:	Being cautious, follows instructions	Esther 2:15-22
2- PERSONAL GIFTEDNESS:	Attention to details, validation, loyal, follows the rules, diplomatic	Luke 1:1-4 Esther 4:15-16; 5:1-4
3- INSTINCTIVE FEARS:	The unknown or undefined	Esther 4:10-17
4- BLIND SPOT:	Being too cautious and concerned with details	Esther 5:5-8, Esther 7:1-10

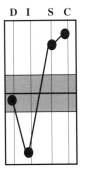

C/S/D   **Moses, Thomas*, Naomi***

1- PRIMARY DRIVE:	Doing things right, being accurate	Exodus 24:1-18
2- PERSONAL GIFTEDNESS:	Steadiness in completing the assigned task	Deut. 1:3; 4:1 Deut. 5:1; 6:1; 8:1
3- INSTINCTIVE FEARS:	Criticism directed toward them	Numbers 11:10-15
4- BLIND SPOTS:	Unrealistic expectations cause them to decline promising opportunities	Exodus 3:7-22; 4:1-13 John 20:24-29

C/S/I   **Elijah, Deborah *, Ruth ***

1- PRIMARY DRIVE:	Intense desire to maintain quality	I Kings 18:1-19
2- PERSONAL GIFTEDNESS:	Conscientious in communicating quality standards	I Kings 18:21-40 Judges 4, 5
3- INSTINCTIVE FEARS:	Criticism of personal effort or work	I Kings 19:2-4
4- BLIND SPOTS:	Incongruency of feelings making logical thinking impossible	I Kings 19:9-14

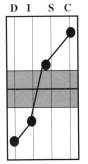

C/S   **John, Mary ***

1- PRIMARY DRIVE:	Compliant, cooperative	Luke 1:26-38
2- PERSONAL GIFTEDNESS:	Team player, good follow-through, dependable, and conscientious	Luke 1:39-56 John 19:26-27
3- INSTINCTIVE FEARS:	Surprises and illogical thinking	Luke 1:28-34
4- BLIND SPOTS:	Being preoccupied with having to resolve every experience logically	Luke 2:7-19

* Tendencies indicate a pattern, but not enough Scriptural content to make a confident association.

High C Discovery Exercise

In your opinion, how is the High C different from the High D, the High I, and the High S?

What are some observable differences in the High C Representative Patterns?

Pure C

C/S/D

C/S/I

C/S

High C's are sensitive to criticism and can express feeling of being all alone in their problem. Left unchecked, they can experience depression and even have thoughts of suicide.

Read I Kings 18:16-40; 19:21. Describe the contest Elijah proposed to Ahab and the priests of Baal. How did the contest conclude?

In I Kings 19, how did Jezebel feel toward Elijah? How did Elijah respond? What did he want to do? What does Elijah's behavior reflect High C tendencies?

A Look Ahead

In the next lesson we will look at what causes High C's to react to pressure the way they do. In addition, we will suggest ways you can help them. Finally, we will study the way God dealt with Moses, helping him become His spokesman to Pharaoh.

RESPONDING TO THE NEEDS OF THE COMPLIANCE PERSONALITY

Assignment:
Understanding How Others Miunderstand You,
textbook chapter 12, pages 227-250

If you are to understand how to love the High C, you must first understand what happens to a High C when certain of his needs are not met. High C's desire a controlled, defined work environment that offers reassurance and security. Because God has given High C's perfectionist tendencies and expectations, they can be very hard on themselves. High C's tend to personalize negative information and are extremely sensitive to criticism.

Whereas the High D becomes aggressively intense if he is criticized, the High C becomes introspective. Whereas criticism may cause the High I to become emotional and attack, it causes the High C to become quiet and stoic. Whereas the High S retreats into a shell when he is criticised, the High C may have a total self-image breakdown. All these responses are predictable and normal for the respective profiles when they encounter criticism.

In this lesson we will study the situations that commonly cause High C profiles to respond in the manner outlined above. In addition, we will look at a biblical case study in which Israel criticized the Lord and Moses, a High C.

Most important, we will look at what elements are necessary to give the High C the best chance to handle situations that are stressful for him. In addition, we will review a biblical case study in which God created a specific environment for Moses so that he had the opportunity to begin the process of dealing with these issues. Finally, through a series of questions designed for small group discussion you will be given the opportunity to test the concepts presented in the lesson.

Understanding High C Stress

Need Issues: • Order and defined responsibility
 • Reassurance of support

The High C begins to encounter stress when:

1. Someone changes his plans and/or criticizes the High C's work
2. The change in plans commonly causes the High C to ask many "what about" and "what if " questions
3. Continued criticism causes feelings of hopelessness, inadequacy, and being totally alone
4. If the High C's partner becomes impatient with the continuous reservoir of questions and projects a critical spirit, the High C has a tendency to take it personally
5. The High C can also have a total self-image breakdown, a "poor me" attitude, and /or even thoughts of suicide

Biblical Case Study: Numbers 11:1-15

Read the Scripture passage and describe how some of the people felt about the food God provided for them. Describe Moses' response to their complaints. What did he do? What was his solution to the problem? What C tendencies are present?

Understanding the High C Environment

- **HOW TO RESPOND TO A HIGH C**
- Be specific and accurate
- Make allowances for initial responses to be cautious and/or negative
- Allow freedom to ask questions

- **HOW TO RELATE TO A HIGH C**
- Answer questions in a patient and persistent manner
- Mix accurate data with assurances of how you will offer support
- Allow time to process data

- **HOW TO REINFORCE THE HIGH C**
- Provide a step-by-step approach to goal
- Provide reassurance of support
- Give permission to validate data with third parties they respect

Assignment

If you know a High C, have him review the list above. Have him pick a least one element that is important and meaningful in creating a loving environment for him. Record his response below.

Optional Exercise

To me, the most interesting element of the High C environment is:

84

Understanding God's style of loving Moses

Read Exodus 3:1-4:31. In the left column, are the critical verses of the passage which describe God's actions and Moses' reactions. In the right column, describe in your own words the environment that God created as He spoke to Moses. How does it compare to the suggestions listed on the previous page in loving the High C?

God's Actions and Moses' Reactions	Your insights into God's environment
"And the angel of the Lord appeared to him in a blazing..bush.... And [God] said, 'Moses, Moses!" And he said, 'Here I am.'... Then He said...I am the God of your father, the God of Abraham, the God of Isaac, and the God of Jacob.' Then Moses hid his face, for he was afraid... And the Lord said, 'I have surely seen the affliction of My people who are in Egypt...Therefore, come now, and I will send you to Pharaoh, so that you may bring My people, the sons of Israel, out of Egypt.' But Moses said to God, 'Who am I, that should go to Pharoah?... And He said, 'Certainly I will be with you, and ... you shall worship God at this mountain.'	Describe how did God initially introduce Himself to Moses? In your opinion, did He provide enough information to communicate who He was?
Then Moses said to God, 'What shall I say to them? God said ...I AM WHO I AM. Then Moses answered, 'What if they will not believe me.' [*And the Lord gave him three signs: his staff turning into a serpent, his hand turning leprous and back to normal and a promise to turn the Nile River to blood.*] Then Moses said to the Lord, 'Please Lord,...I am slow of speech. The Lord said to him, '...I will be with your mouth and teach you what to say. But he said, ' Please, Lord send the message by whomever Thou wilt.' Then Moses departed and returned to Jethro his father-in-law, and said to him, 'Please let me go back...to Egypt.' And Jethro said to Moses, 'Go in peace.'"	How did God respond when Moses asked questions? After his conversation with God and before he returned to Egypt, what did Moses do? Why do you think he did this?

DISCovering the High C:
Worksheet for High C Profiles

This worksheet and the worksheet that immediately follows go together and should be discussed by specific groups. High C profiles should use this worksheet; Low C profiles (D's, I's, and S's) should use the worksheet on the next page.

After all questions have been answered, share your answers with your partner, discussing your responses to question 1, then question 2, and so on. If you are using a discussion group method, select a spokesman to share the consensus of the group's findings. Then join the other three profiles for the group discussion.

1a.   If I had to describe my behavior in three phrases, I would choose the following words...

1b.   I like jobs that have tasks which involve...

1c.   But I would rather delegate tasks that are involved with...

2.   If I had to select three components from the list on page 84 to better respond, relate and reinforce me, they would be...

3.   As I reflect on how God responded to Moses, He would also have ministered to me when He...

4a.   When I am under stress, the most loving thing you can do for me is

4b.   I have learned to overcome my need for the status quo by...

5.   In order to develop better relationships with the other profiles, I continually need to work on the following areas of my behavioral style:

in relating to the High D

in relating to the High I

in relating to the High S

Loving the High C:
<u>Worksheet for Low C profiles</u>

This worksheet is to be filled out by the Low C profiles (D's, I's, and S's) at the same time the High C's are filling out their worksheet. After you have answered all of the questions, share your answers. If you are using a discussion group method, divide into at least three groups (High D's, High I's, and High S's) and select a spokesman for each group. Rejoin the high C's and share the consensus of the group's findings, discussing one question at a time, alternating between the High C worksheet and the Low C worksheet.

1.   Areas of my life where I need the gifts of the High C:

2.   As I reflect on the ways to respond, relate, and reinforce the High C listed on page 84, the most difficult component for me to create and communicate is:

3.   The one component God used in communicating with Moses, that I need to work on in relating to a High C is:

4.   As I review my differences in styles with the High C, I see my greatest potential for conflict to be:

because

5.   In order to build a better personal and working relationship with High C's, I need to be willing to modify my need to/for:

Bonus Question:

6.   If I were planning a date or function with a High C , I would include the following activities:

MEASURING THE MATURITY OF DISC PROFILES

Assignment:
Understanding How Others Misunderstand You,
textbook, chapter 13, pages 250-265

Matthew 22:37

And He said to him, **" You shall love the Lord your God with all your heart, and with all your soul, and with all your mind."**

One of the measurements of a person's maturity is how well he handles stress in a way that is contrary to his nature's negative bent. Normally, making such an adjustment requires of the person that he make a choice between his need system and his value system. The difference between a need system response and a value system response will be discussed in this session along with biblical examples.

This final session will be devoted to explaining how positive changes can take place with the DISC models. The testimonies will be those of Peter, Paul, Abraham, and Moses, showing how they successfully handled stress issues that earlier in their lives had caused them to fail. This same potential is available to us all.

Differences in Needs and Values

Clarifying the differences between our needs-motivated behavior and our values-motivated behavior further identifies the way each person understands himself and others.

Needs-motivated Behavior	Values-motivated Behavior[1]
What is most natural for us	What others and/or we expect of us
The "would do's" of living	The "should do's" of living
What is most pleasurable	What is right
What we feel is easiest	What we think is best
What is most practical	What is most meaningful

Needs-motivated behavior has to do with the behavior that is easiest and most natural for us. It is the type of behavior dealt with in the DISC system used in this workbook and the accompanying text. Values-motivated behavior has to do with what we think is right, reasonable, and meaningful, and what we believe others expect from us.

Identify the following situations as involving needs-or values-motivated conflict. Place an _N_ on the line for a nees-motivated conflict and a _V_ on the line for a values-motivated conflict.

1. A person fails to meet a deadline on a project despite a genuine effort to complete it. _____

2. A Christian education director changes his Sunday School attendance report to the pastor inorder to reach the church's published high attendance goal.

    _____

3. A manager with an organized and goal-oriented mind has difficulty meeting the same standards he demands from others. _____

4. A colleague promises to support your position in a job dispute but sides with the boss, who expresses the need for a different course of action. _____

---

1. <u>Values Model Encyclopedia</u>, Life Associates, Inc., Bonita Springs, FL

Measuring the Maturity of the High D

Fears of the High D • **Loss of control and disclosure of weakness**

Defensive response • **Use of anger and force to regain control and cover up weaknesses**

Case study: Paul (2 Corinthians 12: 7-10)

In this passage, Paul highlights several conversations with the Lord regarding an apparent weakness that he had. His goal was to be healed. God disagreed. The normal High D response would be to become angry with God and try to regain control of the situation by refusing to serve until something positive was done about it. Contrast Paul's response to God concerning his thorn in the flesh with the natural fears of the High D. **What risks do you see Paul taking?**

"And because of the surpassing greatness of the revelations, for this reason, to keep me from exalting myself, there was given me a thorn in the flesh, a messenger of Satan to buffet--to keep me from exalting myself!

Concerning this I entreated the Lord three times that it might depart from me.

And He has said to me, 'My grace is sufficient for you, for power is perfected in weakness. Most gladly, therefore, I will rather boast about my weakness, that the power of Christ may dwell in men.'

Therefore, I am well content with weaknesses, with insults, with distresses, with persecutions, with difficulties, for Christ's sake; for when I am weak, then I am strong."

Measuring the Maturity of the High I

Fears of the High I   • Loss of social acceptance and self-worth.

Defensive response   • Use of verbal skills to justify actions by using shift blame strategies

Case study: Peter (Acts 4:7-12)

Peter was on trial for his life. Contrast Peter's response to the Sanhedrin and his need to be accepted by this important body. His High I profile would ordinarily demand that he use his verbal skills to resolve the issues so that the council would find him innocent. Contrast Peter's actions with the typical High I fears. **What risk did Peter take?**

"And when they had placed them in the center, they began to inquire, 'By what power, or in what name, have you done this?'

Then Peter, filled with the Holy Spirit, said to them, 'Ruler and elders of the people,

if we are on trial today for a benefit done to a sick man, as to how this man has been made well,

let it be known to all of you, and to all the people of Israel, that by the name of Jesus Christ the Nazarene, who you crucified, whom God raised from the dead--by this <u>name</u> this man stands here before you in good health.

'He is the STONE WHICH WAS REJECTED by you, THE BUILDERS, but WHICH BECAME THE VERY CORNER STONE.'

And there is salvation in no one else; for there is no other name under heaven that has been given among men, by which we must be saved.' "

Measuring the Maturity of the High S

Fears of the High S • **Giving up security and facing conflict**

Defensive response • **Maintain status quo and avoid pain by employing a passive-aggressive strategy**

Case study: Abraham (Genesis 22:1-3, 9-10)

In this passage, God asks Abraham to offer up his son Isaac. The normal response of a High S is to become busy doing other things and ignore the message. If pushed on the issue, High S's would be likely to suggest a compromise but avoid making a decision. Contrast the actions of Abraham with the natural fears of the High S. **What risk do you see Abraham taking?**

"Now it came about after these things, that God tested Abraham, and said to him, 'Abraham!' And he said, 'Here I am.'

And He said, 'Take now your son, your only son, whom you love, Isaac, and go to the land of Moriah; and offer him there as a burnt offering on one of the mountains of which I will tell you.'

So Abraham rose early in the morning and saddled his donkey, and took two of his young men with him and Isaac his son; and he split wood for the burnt offering, and arose and went to the place of which God had told him.

Then they came to the place of which God had told him; and Abraham built the altar there, and arranged the wood, and bound his son Isaac, and laid him on the altar on top of the wood.

And Abraham stretched out his hand, and took the knife to slay his son."

Measuring the Maturity of the High C

Fears of the High C
- Making unpopular decisions alone, creating antagonism, the unknown.

Defensive response
- Move cautiously, ask lots of questions, and use a "poor me" strategy as a means of not getting involved

Case study: Moses (Exodus 32: 9-10, 30-32)

In this passage, God commanded Moses to independently confront Israel with its great sin of worshipping the golden calf. By using a pro and con strategy, God guided Moses toward committing himself to the assignment. However, when Moses personally saw the Israelites in the midst of this grievous sin, it was obvious someone would have to go back up to God and make an atonement for it. The normal High C response would be to pray about it for several weeks, select a committee to carry the message, and ask someone else to be the spokesman. Contrast Moses response to the fears of the High C. **What risks did Moses take?**

"And the Lord said to Moses, 'I have seen this people, and behold, they are an obstinate people.

Now then let Me alone, that My anger may burn against them, and that I may destroy them; and I will make of you a great nation.'

And it came about on the next day that Moses said to the people, 'You yourselves have committed a great sin; and now I am going up to the Lord, perhaps I can make atonement for your sin.

Then Moses returned to the Lord, and said, 'Alas, this people has committed a great sin, and they have made a god of gold for themselves.

But now, if Thou wilt, forgive their sin--and if not, please blot me out from Thy book which Thou hast written!' "

Worksheet

1. What risk did each of the biblical characters have to face as it related to his natural fear?

    Paul, High D:

    Peter, High I:

    Abraham, High S:

    Moses, High C:

2. Put yourself in the place of the biblical character most like you. Describe how you would have reacted.

3. If you had to list your greatest fear, what would it be?

    High D group :

    High I group :

    High S group:

    High C group:

4. If you had to face this fear, what would you recommend we do to help you?

Appendix Exercises

Appendix A   Spiritual Gifts & Profiles

Appendix B   Acts 15 team profiles

Appendix C   Profiling a marriage

Appendix D   Person profile of Jesus

Appendix E   Resources

Spiritual Gifts and Behavior Styles

Is it possible that a relationship exists between spiritual gifts and behavior styles?

I Corinthians 12: 4-7

Now there are varieties of gifts, but the same Spirit.

And there are varieties of ministries and same Lord.

And there are varieties of effects, but the same God who works all things in all persons.

But to each one is given the manifestation of the Spirit for the common good."

There appears to be some loose correlation between specific behavior profiles and clusters of certain spiritual gifts. It is does not mean that God exclusively holds to these trends. On the contrary, the Lord is sovereign and He can and does give spiritual gifts according to His will. However, if an individual is given a spiritual gift not commonly found among a specific pattern, the type of ministry and the effect of that ministry will be very different than is normally associated with that gift. Although many spiritual gift instruments are available, feedback from the body of Christ is the best method of validating your gifts.

This exercise's purpose is to stimulate your thinking into putting together your behavior style with your gifts. The next two pages contain a partial listing of spiritual gifts commonly associated with specific representative behavior patterns. It is not intended to be a complete list but is designed to be a framework to more clearly define where you can best serve the body of Christ.

Circle the pattern, Biblical model and spiritual gifts that best describes you.

DISC Blends	Biblical Model	Potential Gifts/Ministries
Primary D - p.135	Solomon, Rahab (*) (I Kings 3:5-14)	Wisdom, Exhortation, Administration
D/I - p.135	Joshua, Sarah (*) (Joshua 1)	Leadership, Exhortation Faith
D equal I - p.136	Stephen, Lydia (*) (Acts 7)	Prophecy, Evangelism, Teaching
D/C - p.136	Paul, Michal (*) (Acts 16:16-18)	Discernment, Wisdom Prophecy
Primary I - p.137	Aaron, King Saul (Exodus 4:27-31)	Helps, Hospitality, Mercy,
I/D - p.137	Peter, Rebekah (Acts 2:14-41)	Evangelism, Hospitality, Exhortation
I/S- p.138	Barnabas, Abigail (Acts 4:36-37; I Sam. 25:14-31)	Giving, Helps, Pastor-Teacher
I/C - p.138	David, Mary Magdalene (*) (I Sam. 17:26-54; 25:32-35)	Faith, Leadership, Mercy
Primary S - p.139	Isaac, Dorcas(*) (Acts 9:36-39)	Helps, Service, Mercy
S/D - p.139	Nehemiah, Joseph, Martha (*) (Neh. 2:1-18; Gen. 39:1-6)	Administration, Service Leadership
S/I - p.140	Abraham, Hannah (Gen. 15:1-5; Gen. 18:1-6)	Faith, Hospitality, Mercy
S/C/D - p.140	Jacob, Anna (*) (Gen. 29:14-20; Gen. 30:27-43)	Service, Helps, Wisdom
Primary C - p.141	Luke, Esther (Gospel of Luke)	Pastor-Teacher, Helps, Service
C/S/D - p.141	Moses, Thomas (*), Naomi (*) (Book of Deuteronomy)	Pastor-Teacher, Exhortation, Leadership
C/I/S - p.142	Elijah, Deborah (*), Ruth (*) (I Kings 18)	Exhortation, Helps, Knowledge
C/S - p.142	John, Mary (*) (Gospel of John, I, II, III, John)	Knowledge, Teaching, Service

Handwritten annotations in left margin:
- Doug private (next to Primary D)
- Aaron (next to D equal I)
- Peggy (next to Primary S)
- Russell (next to S/D)
- Doug-projected (next to S/I)
- Kathy (next to C/S/D)

Used by permission of In His Grace, Inc.

Spiritual Gifts/Ministries and Their Short Definitions

Administration- The God-given ability to make decisions and give direction in such a way that others can efficiently and effectively accomplish their goals.

Discernment- The God-given ability to be able to determine whether what was spoken or done was of Satan or of God.

Exhortation- The God-given ability to encourage people to act on the word of God in their time of need, persuading them to take courage and comfort in what they must do.

Evangelist- The ministry which results from God combining appropriate spiritual gifts and your behavior profile to create your ministry to unbelievers.

Faith- The God-given ability to recognize in a situation what God intends to do, and live a life that demonstrates a genuine and solid trust in God to bring it to pass.

Giving- The God-given ability to unselfishly, joyfully, and eagerly share your material resources with others.

Helps- The God-given ability to unselfishly, joyfully, and eagerly support or relieve others in the performing of a task.

Hospitality- The God-given ability to unselfishly, joyfully, and eagerly entertain strangers or guests in your home.

Knowledge- The God-given ability to grasp spiritual truth which others could not understand on their own.

Leadership- The God-given ability to meet the needs of people by helping them to accomplish their goals.

Mercy- The God-given ability to demonstrate immediate compassion to those who are suffering.

Pastor-Teacher- The ministry which results from God combining appropriate spiritual gifts and your behavior profile to create your ministry to believers.

Prophecy- The God-given ability to proclaim the word of God, edifying the believer and convicting the unbeliever.

Teaching- The God-given ability to explain the truth of God's word in an understandable and relevant way.

Service- The God-given ability to cheerfully and eagerly assist in the performing of a task that benefits the practical needs of others.

Wisdom- The God-given ability to have insight into people and situations that is not obvious to the average person, and knowing how to respond in a Godly way.

Personal Skills, Gifts and Passion Worksheet

I believe my individual and team skills are:

I perceive my spiritual gift(s) are:

My ministry passion is:

The ministries/jobs I have had but do not feel called are:

I perceive my limitations are:

The skills I need on my team to offset my limitations are:

The behavior patterns that best represent these skills are:

I best respond in an environment that includes:

When I am under stress or conflict, the best thing you can do to help me is:

ACTS 15 TEAM EXERCISE

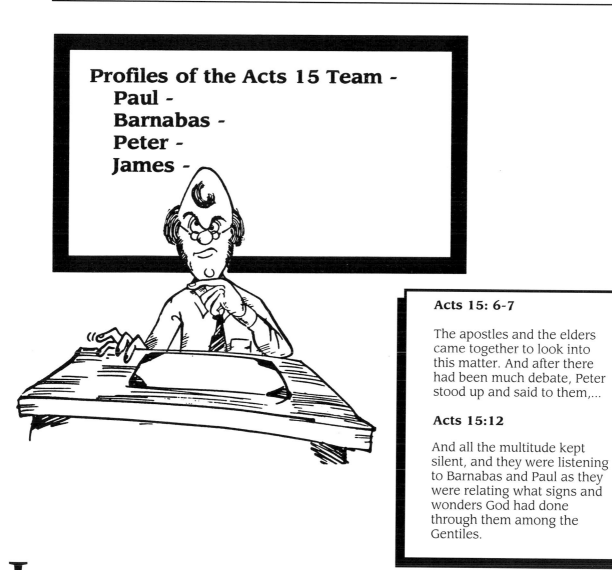

Profiles of the Acts 15 Team -
  Paul -
  Barnabas -
  Peter -
  James -

Acts 15: 6-7

The apostles and the elders came together to look into this matter. And after there had been much debate, Peter stood up and said to them,...

Acts 15:12

And all the multitude kept silent, and they were listening to Barnabas and Paul as they were relating what signs and wonders God had done through them among the Gentiles.

It is vital to understand the skills and functions of individual team members. It is also necessary for the team members to know each other and use each other's gifts. However, before a team can become truly effective, the members must know how to respect each other and work together. The purpose of this exercise is to show a biblical team with different skills working together to solve a difficult problem. Later, they will have yet another problem, and fail.

Your assignment will be to determine the different skills found in the four major characters: Paul, Barnabas, Peter, and James. You will be asked to observe how their personality skills were used to resolve the major issue before the council in Acts 15. You will also study why their styles came into conflict in Galatians 2:11-14 and at the end of Acts 15.

Acts 15 Team

Read Acts 15, observing the reaction of the leaders in the church. After studying each response, turn to the worksheet and discuss the questions.

Paul
D/C Profile

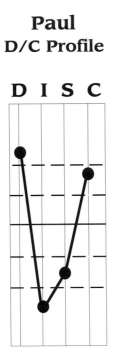

Barnabas
I/S Profile

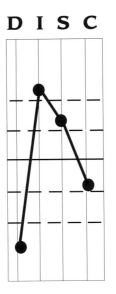

Peter
I/D Profile

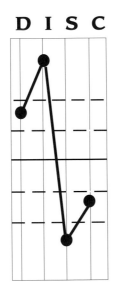

James
S/C/D Profile

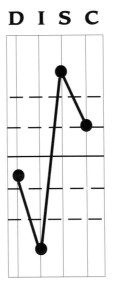

Acts 15 Profiles

Paul - D/C

Primary Drive	Enjoys aggression; may be limited in verbal skills
Goal	To control; unique accomplishments
Judges Others by	Personal standards; getting things done; commitment to their goals
Personal Giftedness	Setting a pace in developing systems; task or project competition
Group Giftedness	Initiate or create change in thinking; critical, systematic problem solver
Instinctively fears	Not being influential or in control; people failing to achieve their standards
Under stress becomes	Cold, uncaring, blunt, critical, and condescending
Under pressure becomes	Bored with routine work; uncooperative and sulky when unwillingly constrained; assertive and pioneering
Needs to work on	Warmth and tact in communicating with others; awareness that rules can also apply to them

Barnabas - I/S

Primary Drive	Is to gain acceptance of self and others; affectionate and understanding
Goal	Friendship; harmony
Judges others by	Positive acceptance; generally looking for good in people
Personal Giftedness	Encouraging others; practicing an "open door" policy
Group Giftedness	Stability; wide range of friendships; good at listening to feelings
Instinctively fears	Pressuring people; being accused of causing harm; experiencing disharmony
Under stress becomes	Tolerant; will compromise in order to restore harmony
Under pressure becomes	Becomes overly flexible and intimate; too trusting of others
Needs to work on	Being realistic about deadlines; remaining focused in getting the task done

Peter - I/D

Primary Drive	Being enthusiastic; being spontaneous
Goal	Being in charge; being associated with something that is important; status symbols
Judges others by	Their ability to verbalize their thoughts; being unstructured and flexible
Personal Giftedness	Friendly manner; openness; verbal and nonverbal adeptness
Group Giftedness	Ability to communicate and bring closure; abundance of poise, confidence
Instinctively fears	A fixed or structured environment; complex situations or relationships
Under stress becomes	Too optimistic and oversells; reckless and verbally unstable
Under pressure becomes	Becomes soft and persuadable, particularly if social choices come into play
Needs to work on	Remaining focused on tasks; attention to key details; becoming too overconfident

James - S/C/D

Primary Drive	Remaining focused in the completing the task; self-disciplined
Goal	Commitment to the chain of command
Judges others by	Use of logic and data
Personal Giftedness	Determination, tenacity; never gives up
Group Giftedness	Attention to details, being comprehensive; working on tasks individually or in small groups
Instinctively fears	Loss of security and discounting of traditions
Under stress becomes	Blunt, direct, and insensitive; suspicion of others and their motives
Under pressure becomes	Worrisome; tends to internalize conflict; remembers wrongs done to them in detail
Needs to work on	Being more flexible; personal involvement with others

Acts 15 Worksheet

Describe the behavioral differences of the four major characters: Paul, Barnabas, Peter, and James.

Prior to and during the council, what contribution did each make in moving toward a solution? (Describe the contribution by naming a skill.)

Describe and contrast any behavioral differences among the major characters.

Later in Antioch (scripture references - Galatians 2:11-14, Acts 15:36-40), what issues caused them to disagree?

Why?

CREATING LOVING ENVIRONMENTS

What profile would make the best marriage partner for me?

"This is My commandment, that you love one another, just as I have loved you." **Jesus** John 15:12

"Make my joy complete by being of the same mind, maintaining the same love, united in spirit, intent on one purpose.
  Do nothing from selfishness or empty conceit, but with humility of mind let each of you regard one another as more important than himself;
  do not merely look out for your own personal interests, but also for the interests of others. **Paul**

Philippians 2:2-4

One of the most frequent questions asked about profile styles relates to marriage compatibility. It is important to remember that the profiles of two people are not what determine a relationship's success; success comes from a couple's commitment and attitudes. Any couple, regardless of profiles, can be incompatible just as any couple can learn how to meet one another's needs.

This exercise will help you and your partner learn how to communicate your needs, and your love, to each other. Don't be surprised if your needs are very different from your partner's. The discovery is part of the excitement which comes as you learn to maximize your relationship.

Analysis of
PARTNER PROFILES

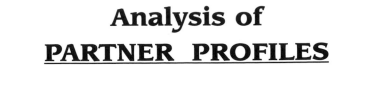

My Profile: My Partner's Profile:

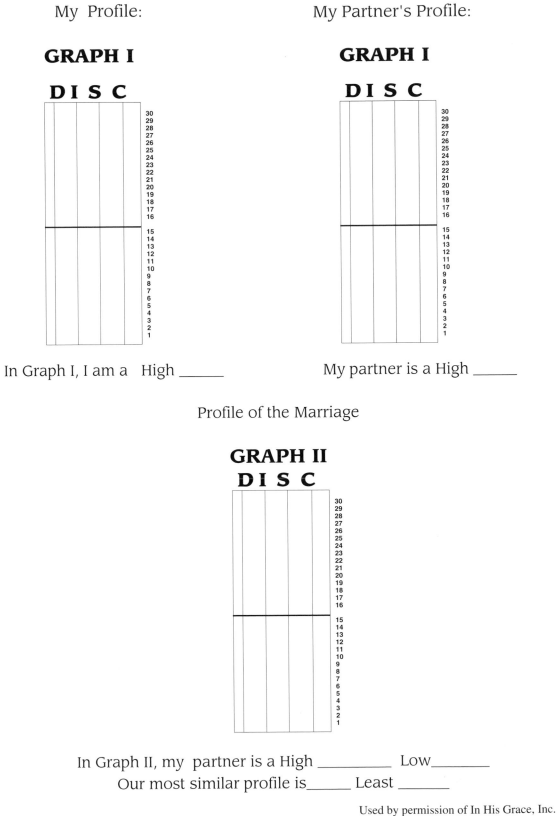

GRAPH I

D I S C

In Graph I, I am a   High _____   My partner is a High _____

Profile of the Marriage

GRAPH II
D I S C

In Graph II, my partner is a High _____ Low_____
Our most similar profile is_____ Least _____

Used by permission of In His Grace, Inc.

Comparisons of DISC Profiles

Assignment: Draw a *square* around the High style which describes you
and a *circle* around your partner's; compare the differences.

[handwritten annotations: Doug / Aaron Russell Aaron / Peggy me Russell / me]

High D Characteristics	High I Characteristics	High S Characteristics	High C Characteristics
Tendencies	*Tendencies*	*Tendencies*	*Tendencies*
quick action, creating change, taking charge, getting results	verbalizing, generating enthusiasm	sitting or staying in one place, demonstrating patience	following directions and maintaining standards, checking for accuracy
Desired environment	*Desired environment*	*Desired environment*	*Desired environment*
freedom from controls and supervision, many varied activities	social recognition, popularity, freedom from control and detail	sincere appreciation, traditional procedures, known results	no sudden or abrupt changes, security reassurances
Motivating needs	*Motivating needs*	*Motivating needs*	*Motivating needs*
challenges, power, and authority	flexibility, freedom of speech	stability, time to adjust to change	be part of a group, time to analyze
Fears	*Fears*	*Fears*	*Fears*
being taken advantage of	loss of social recognition	confrontation, change	irrational acts, antagonism
Judges others by	*Judges others by*	*Judges others by*	*Judges others by*
aggressiveness, results	verbal skills, flexibility	consistency, amiableness	accuracy, precise standards
Stress release	*Stress release*	*Stress release*	*Stress release*
open hostility	emotional expression of feelings	excessive need for sleep	need for time alone
Recovery needs	*Recovery needs*	*Recovery needs*	*Recovery needs*
physical time	social time	"nothing" time	quiet time

Used by permission of In His Grace, Inc.

Communicating Differences

I feel the four best words to describe my strengths and weaknesses are:

As I reviewed my personal profile, I feel the one outstanding trait or skill I most relate to is:

I feel I need to improve on:

The one area I need help from someone else is :

If I could select key elements to incorporate in a loving environment for me, they would be:

Share your environment needs with your partner.   Our greatest difference is my need for _____

and their need for _____

When I am under stress, the most loving thing you can do for me is to

_____

My partner's response was to _____

THE PERSONAL PROFILE OF JESUS

Assignment:

Understanding How Others Misunderstand You,

textbook, chapter 14, pages 266-282

> **John 11:33-36**
>
> **33** When Jesus therefore saw her weeping...He was deeply moved in spirit, and was troubled.
> **34** "Where have you laid him?" He asked.
> "Come and see, Lord," they replied.
> **35** Jesus wept.
> **36** And so the Jews were saying, "Behold how He loved him!"

One of the most frequent questions asked is, "What was the personal profile of Jesus?" To answer the question, one must first arrive at a position on who He was. Jesus claimed to be God, the Son of Man. Those in His hometown reasoned He was insane. The religious leaders, the Pharisees, testified before Pilate that Jesus had to be a liar. After spending three years with Him, Peter, John, and the disciples concluded that He had to be the Son of God. Scripture records that Satan and the demons agreed with the disciples. Finally, of the three recorded New Testament statements by God the Father, two directly confirm that Jesus was His Son. What is important is for you to discover who He was.

In studying the behavior of Christ, we will first look at Graph I, which deals with who Jesus was in a given circumstance. This graph typically varies depending upon the expectation of those involved. The ideal, of course, is for the individual to take on the behavioral style that best meets the need of the situation. To validate Jesus' profile for yourself, study the Scripture references on page 114 which correlate to the traits found on the DISC Trait Continuums on page 23 of this workbook. What does this tell you about His ability to adapt to the need of any given situation?

DISC Trait Continuums

High D Dominance **Comfortable working independently**	High I Influence **Comfortable working with people**	High S Steadiness **Comfortable working in a routine**	High C Compliance **Comfortable working in a defined system**	
Mark 5:1-13 Luke 4:8 domineering dictatorial Mark 1:21-27	Matt. 14:14 persuasive spontaneous Matt. 14:16-21 Matt. 14:24-33	patient Mark 14:26-31 steady Luke 22:31-32 Luke 22:54-61	perfectionistic Luke 4:3-4 accurate Luke 4:12 Matt. 4:5-12	**30 29 28 27 26**
Luke 4:41 Luke 8:23-25 risk-taker Luke 11:38-54 Matt. 12:10-14 self-assured Mark 12:38-40	John 4:11-30 John 3:1-21 John 4:5-10 Luke 11:37 sociable Luke 10:38-42 charitable	John 21:15-19 John 20:19-31 John 8:1-11 John 4:4-9 Mark 4:1-2 good listener Luke 10: 1-11	Luke 9:14-17 thorough Matt. 26:50-56 restrained Mark 14:55-61 John 19:7-11 Luke 19:41-44	25 24 23 22 21 20 19
Mark 11:27-33 Matt. 22:23-46 John 15:1-17	Mark 8: 1-9 Matt. 8:1-14 Matt. 19:1-2	deliberate amiable Matt.19:13-15	sensitive John 11:32-35 Mark 6:34	**18 17 16**
Matt.12:14-21 Mark 7:24 Mark 5:38-43	convincing Luke 9:18-35 John 4:31-42	mobile Matt. 15:29-30 Matt. 19: 1-2	"own person" Luke 14:2-4 Luke 15:1-32	**15 14 13**
unassuming Matt. 16:13-21 realistic Mark 9:30-31 Luke 18:31-34 John 8:10-11 mild	Luke 10:25-37 Luke 9:43-44 factual Mark 10:32-34 Matt. 17:22-23 Mark 1:35 Matt. 14:13	Luke 13:22 Matt. 15:1-9 critical of others Matt. 23:1-39 Luke 13:13-16 Luke 7:11-17 Luke 13:10-13	Matt. 16:1-4 Matt. 12:1-8 independent Mark 7:1-8 Luke 19: 45-48 Luke 15:1-2 Mark 3:1-6	12 11 10 9 8 7 6
John 12:27-28 John 6:38-40 Matt. 26:37-42 dependent I Cor. 15:27-28	Luke 22:41 Luke 6:12 withdrawn Matt. 14:22-23 probing	Luke 5:1-3 intense spontaneous Luke 5:4-11 Matt 13:1-9	Mark 2:23-28 rebellious Luke 19:1-7 fearless Matt. 9:9-13	5 4 3 2 1
Comfortable working on a team **Low D** Dominance	**Comfortable working alone** **Low I** Influence	**Comfortable working with no structure** **Low S** Steadiness	**Comfortable working with no system** **Low C** Compliance	

Used by permission of In His Grace, Inc.

110

Christ's profiles in Graphs II and III

GRAPH II
Private concept:

D I S C

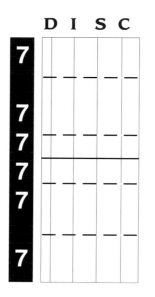

Graph II is most indicative of who a person really is. If Jesus was God, He had to be perfect. Since the number seven represents perfection, the segment numbers were changed to indicate His Deity. However, you decide how well Jesus responded to pressure by studying the Scripture references below.

High D - John 8:12-59
Low D - Matt. 26:36-56, John 17

High I - John 4:1-42
Low I - Matt. 4:1-11

High S - John 8:1-9, Luke 22:31-34
Low S - John 2:12-17, Matt. 21:12-17

High C - Matt. 22:23-46
Low C - Matt. 12:1-14

GRAPH III

Public Concept

D I S C

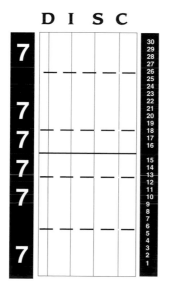

The third graph describes a person's public concept. When asked, Jesus preferred the title "Son of Man," indicating a combination of God and Man. To indicate this on Graph III, the segment numbers on the left retain the number seven, confirming His Diety and the DISC traits numbers on the right (1-30), His humanity; i.e.,100 per cent God and 100 per cent man. To further your understanding of Jesus, study the conclusions of those people who knew Him the best. Who do you think Jesus was?

Paul - Phillipians 2:5-11
Peter - Matt. 16:13-16
Demons - Matt. 8:29, Mark 1:24
God the Father - Mark 1:11, Matt. 17:5
John - John 20: 30-31

Used by permission of In His Grace, Inc.

Who was Jesus?

Jesus claimed to be God
(John 8:58)

Two Alternatives

His Claims were FALSE

His Claims were TRUE

HE IS LORD

Two Alternatives

He knew
His claims
were FALSE

He did not
know His claims
were FALSE

He made a
deliberate
misrepre-
sentation

He was
sincerely
deluded

You can
ACCEPT
(John 3:16)

You can
REJECT
(I John 5:12)

He was a
LIAR

He was a
LUNATIC

The opinion
of the
Pharisees
(John 19:21)

The opinion
of those in
His hometown
(Luke 4:22-28)

Based on your personal study, who do you believe Jesus was?

Based on John 3:16, what are the benefits of believing He was the Son of God?

Reprinted by permission from *The Uniqueness of Jesus,* © Campus Crusade for Christ, Inc. 1968.

Profile of the Marriage

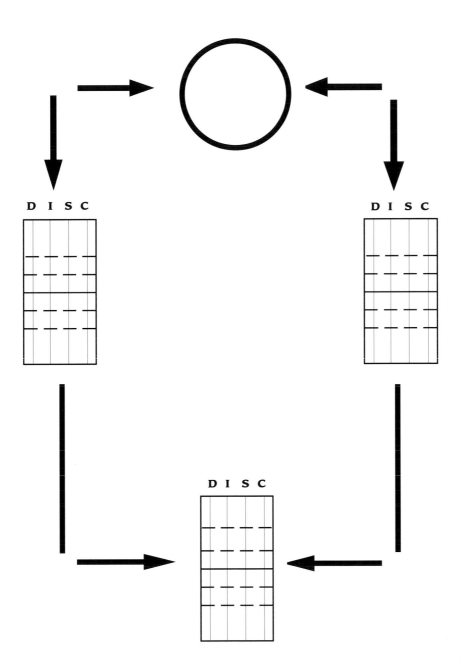

"For this cause a man shall leave his father and his mother, and shall cleave to his wife; and they shall became one flesh."

(Genesis 2:24)

RESOURCES

GENERAL

Ken Voges and Ron Braund. *Understanding How Others Misunderstand You.*
    Chicago: Moody, 1990, Revised 1994.

Ken Voges with Mike Kempainen. *Understanding Jesus, A Personality Profile.*
    Chicago: Moody, 1992.

The Personal DISCernment® Inventory. Team Resources. Atlanta, Georgia, 1991.

The Position DISCernment® Profile. Team Resources, Atlanta, Georgia, 1994.

ADDITIONAL SUPPORT MATERIALS

The *DISC Profile System*™ is a family of instruments and workbooks designed specifically to increase understanding of yourself and others to achieve greater personal and interpersonal effectiveness.

The Personal DISCernment® Inventory is the basic module and offers an opportunity for you to identify your unique temperament. It not only provides a general and detailed description of your particular behavioral style, but it also assists you in developing a comprehensive list of both strengths and weaknesses that help or hinder your effectiveness in various settings.

Also available is a series of application modules that can assist you in applying these insights. The module workbooks listed below provide additional information about each behavioral style in some specific arena as well as suggestions for how you might apply this information to both yourself and teammates. Six application modules are available:

- Team and Temperament
- Time and Temperament
- Task and Temperament

- Management and Temperament
- Marriage Team and Temperament
- Persuasion and Personality

For information on *The DISC Profile System*™ products, contact Team Resources, 5500 Interstate North Parkway, Suite 425 Atlanta, Georgia 30328, (404) 956-0985.

For information on the "Differences in Needs and Values" contact Life Associates, Inc., Bonita Bay Executive Center, 3461 Bonita Bay Blvd., Suite 111 Bonita Springs, FL. 33923, (813)592-1210, Fax (813) 947-3311.

ASSESSMENT INSTRUMENTS AND TECHNICAL SUPPORT

Information on the assessment instruments and training seminars may be obtained from either: AlphaCare, 1827 Powers Ferry Rd., Bldg. 15, Marietta, Georgia 30067, (800) 95-ALPHA, (404) 916-9020, Fax (404) 916-9030 or In His Grace, Inc., 4822 Droddy, Houston, Texas 77091, (713) 688-1201, Fax (713) 681-8466.

Biblical
DISCernment®
Inventory

An Instrument for Understanding Yourself
Through the Lives of Biblical Characters

Biblical **DISC**ernment® Inventory

INCREASING PERSONAL EFFECTIVENESS

Each of us has strengths and weaknesses that make us more effective in some situations and less effective in others. In fact, leadership potential and personal effectiveness are frequently determined by matching strengths against certain situations. And the more closely skills and strengths are aligned with the situation, the *higher* the potential performance.

The ability to predict how we and other people will react and relate in certain situations is of immeasurable value as we attempt to work with, serve, influence, and communicate with others.

Behavior is influenced by a number of complex factors that include basic personality or temperament, current emotional and physical state, our skills, experiences, values, IQ, and motivational needs. These and many other factors play both direct and indirect roles in shaping behavior.

Many of us have discovered that the more we know about ourselves and others, the better we can anticipate behavior in certain situations, and therefore the better we can serve and relate to other people. The Biblical **DISC**ernment® Inventory helps us understand how and why people are likely to behave in one way or another.

We chose the name of this instrument carefully. **DISC**ernment® suggests the means by which we recognize, distinguish, clarify, and gain valuable insight—precisely the purpose of this assessment. The Biblical **DISC**ernment® Inventory will enable you to discover and define how you view yourself and how you want others to see you. And through that process, you will learn more about the *real you*—and what biblical character feels, acts, and thinks like you.

The Biblical **DISC**ernment® Inventory isn't an exam; there are no "right" or "wrong" answers. It is a tool for helping you discover and analyze your own behavioral style, work in an environment that is conducive to your success, and temporarily adapt your behavior to particular situations and create more productive relationships with others.

Biblical **DISC**ernment® Inventory

READ CAREFULLY: In each of the three columns below there are eight four-word groups.
Select two words in each group—*one* which is **MOST** like you and *one* which is **LEAST** like you.
Use a coin to scratch the box next to your choice, and a letter will appear. Please complete all 24
word groups. Then turn the page for scoring instructions.

← Tear to dotted line

Fold down
for scoring

Fold down
for scoring

	Most	Least	**Scratch Test**
EXAMPLE: AUTOCRATIC	X		
CONGENIAL			
STABLE		X	
EXACTING			

Test your coin in the
Scratch Test box.

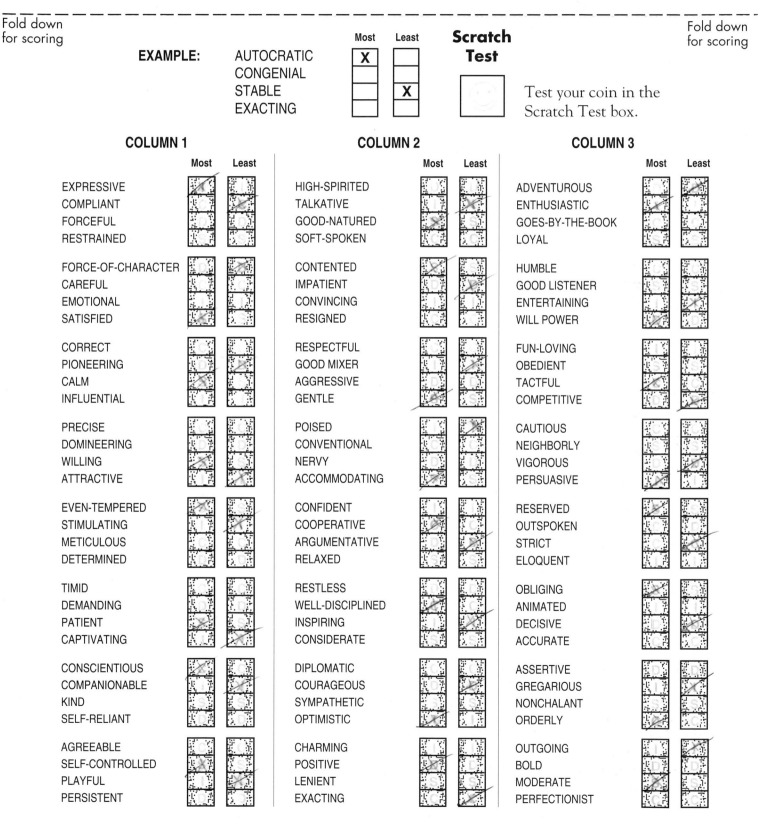

COLUMN 1

EXPRESSIVE
COMPLIANT
FORCEFUL
RESTRAINED

FORCE-OF-CHARACTER
CAREFUL
EMOTIONAL
SATISFIED

CORRECT
PIONEERING
CALM
INFLUENTIAL

PRECISE
DOMINEERING
WILLING
ATTRACTIVE

EVEN-TEMPERED
STIMULATING
METICULOUS
DETERMINED

TIMID
DEMANDING
PATIENT
CAPTIVATING

CONSCIENTIOUS
COMPANIONABLE
KIND
SELF-RELIANT

AGREEABLE
SELF-CONTROLLED
PLAYFUL
PERSISTENT

COLUMN 2

HIGH-SPIRITED
TALKATIVE
GOOD-NATURED
SOFT-SPOKEN

CONTENTED
IMPATIENT
CONVINCING
RESIGNED

RESPECTFUL
GOOD MIXER
AGGRESSIVE
GENTLE

POISED
CONVENTIONAL
NERVY
ACCOMMODATING

CONFIDENT
COOPERATIVE
ARGUMENTATIVE
RELAXED

RESTLESS
WELL-DISCIPLINED
INSPIRING
CONSIDERATE

DIPLOMATIC
COURAGEOUS
SYMPATHETIC
OPTIMISTIC

CHARMING
POSITIVE
LENIENT
EXACTING

COLUMN 3

ADVENTUROUS
ENTHUSIASTIC
GOES-BY-THE-BOOK
LOYAL

HUMBLE
GOOD LISTENER
ENTERTAINING
WILL POWER

FUN-LOVING
OBEDIENT
TACTFUL
COMPETITIVE

CAUTIOUS
NEIGHBORLY
VIGOROUS
PERSUASIVE

RESERVED
OUTSPOKEN
STRICT
ELOQUENT

OBLIGING
ANIMATED
DECISIVE
ACCURATE

ASSERTIVE
GREGARIOUS
NONCHALANT
ORDERLY

OUTGOING
BOLD
MODERATE
PERFECTIONIST

Scoring The Biblical **DISC**ernment® Inventory

COUNTING RESPONSES AND RECORDING

MOST CHOICES

On your answer sheet (page 117), count the number of D's in the "MOST" response columns. Enter your total number of MOST D's in the Scoring Summary Box at the top of page 119, directly beside the "D" and in the column labeled "MOST."

Repeat this procedure to count and record the MOST I's, S's, and C's.

LEAST CHOICES

Now, count the number of times D appears in the response columns labeled "LEAST." Write the total in the Scoring Summary Box beside the "D" in the LEAST column.

Repeat this procedure to count and record the LEAST I's, S's, and C's.

The numbers in each column should total 24.

EXAMPLE 1

	MOST	LEAST	COMPOSITE
D	7	9	
I	10	1	
S	4	6	
C	3	8	
Total	24	24	

COMPUTING THE COMPOSITE

In the Scoring Summary for each category, D, I, S, and C, subtract the number in the LEAST column from the number in the MOST column. Write the difference in the COMPOSITE column.

Use a minus (–) sign if the number in the LEAST column is greater than the number in the MOST column. The COMPOSITE column total should be zero.

EXAMPLE 2

	MOST	LEAST	COMPOSITE
D	7	9	–2
I	10	1	9
S	4	6	–2
C	3	8	–5
Total	24	24	0

PLOTTING YOUR SCORES

Plot your scores on the graphs shown on page 119.

Use the numbers from the MOST column of the Scoring Summary Box to plot the MOST Graph. Circle the number on the "D" Line that corresponds to the number in your Scoring Summary Box. Repeat the process for the I, S, and C numbers in the MOST column. Then connect the dots to form a graph as shown in the example, starting on the "D" column and ending on the "C" column.

Use the numbers from the LEAST column of the Scoring Summary to plot the LEAST Graph.

To plot your scores in the COMPOSITE Graph, use the numbers from the COMPOSITE column of the Scoring Summary Box. Pay particular attention to the plus (+) and minus (–) signs on the COMPOSITE Graph to depict your score accurately—reflecting both highs and lows.

EXAMPLE 3—COMPOSITE

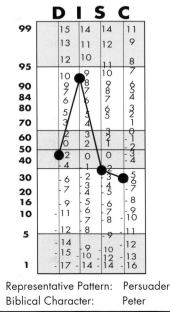

Representative Pattern: Persuader
Biblical Character: Peter

SCORING SUMMARY

	MOST	LEAST	COMPOSITE
D	2	9	-7
I	4	12	-8
S	13	0	+13
C	5	3	+2
Total	24	24	0

Graph your responses as shown in Example 3 on page 118 by **plotting the data from each column in the Scoring Summary Box on the graph of the *same title* below.**

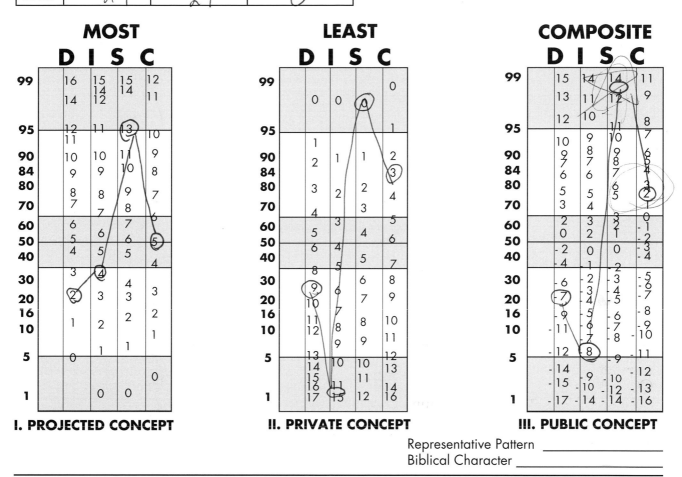

I. PROJECTED CONCEPT

II. PRIVATE CONCEPT

III. PUBLIC CONCEPT

Representative Pattern _____
Biblical Character _____

SEEING BEHAVIOR FROM THREE DIFFERENT PERSPECTIVES

I. Projected Concept (MOST responses): The Projected Concept reflects how you think others want you to behave or how you want them to see you. This is the "mask" people assume in order to achieve success. The roots of your Projected Concept lie in everything you have experienced from childhood to early adulthood—family, friends, schooling, religion. By early adulthood, most people have decided how they must act to get what they want in life, and that behavior becomes their Projected Concept.

II. Private Concept (LEAST responses): This is your basic behavior—what you are down deep. This behavior is a product of heredity and early environment. People display this behavior in relaxed situations (at home or with friends), when they don't sense the need for the "mask" of the Projected Concept, or in stressful situations when maintaining the mask is too difficult.

III. Public Concept (COMPOSITE): The Composite graph represents the net effect of the Private and Projected Concepts and reflects most clearly how others really see you. Note that since the Private (LEAST) Concept is set early in life and the Projected (MOST) Concept is in place by early adulthood, the COMPOSITE is also generally set. As a result, by the time we reach adulthood, deeply-ingrained behavior is very difficult to change.

Biblical **DISC**ernment® Inventory

BACKGROUND OF THE DISC PROFILE SYSTEM™

Dr. William M. Marston, a Columbia University psychologist of the 1920s and 1930s, devised the theory of human behavior on which the Biblical **DISC**ernment® Inventory is based. As a result of extensive research, he identified four major behavioral patterns that are present in all people—but in different degrees. Marston's theory contends that behavior involves an active or passive response to either a favorable or unfavorable environment.

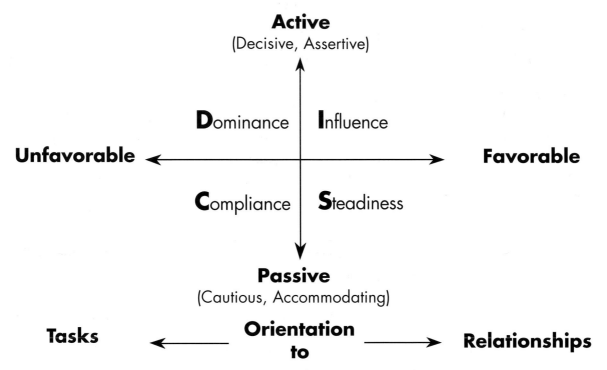

Over the years, many others have built on this four-dimensional theory of personality, making it one of the most popular systems for teaching people about behavioral styles. Today, we call it the DISC Profile System™, and it is based on the following factors:

Dominance: The drive to be in control, to achieve results. The basic intent is to *overcome*.

Influence: The drive to influence, to express, and to be heard. The basic intent is to *persuade*.

Steadiness: The drive to be stable and consistent. The basic intent is to *support*.

Compliance: The drive to be right, sure, and safe. The basic intent is to *avoid trouble*.

In *unfavorable* situations, a person with a high degree of Dominance (D) becomes very active, taking control of the situation to overcome the adversity. On the other hand, a high Compliance (C) individual will react cautiously and try to accommodate the situation in order to stay out of trouble.

In *favorable* situations, the other two elements come to the forefront. A person with a high degree of Influence (I) will respond actively to the environment—motivating, persuading, and interacting energetically with other people. A person with a high Steadiness (S) factor will also relate to others in favorable situations, but in a more low-key manner—being supportive, affirming, and considerate.

For most people, at least two of the four behavioral tendencies appear predominant. For example, a person whose behavioral tendencies lean toward the High D, High I combination will manifest D characteristics in an unfavorable environment and I characteristics when the situation turns favorable. That person will be proactive in either environment but will become more aggressive under stress and more expressive when things are going well.

INTERPRETING THE RESULTS

Although it's important not to stereotype people, it's more risky not to identify and interpret the behavioral characteristics that help us understand ourselves and others.

Using the COMPOSITE Graph for Interpretation

The Biblical **DISC**ernment® Inventory allows us to view our behavior from three different perspectives—the Projected (MOST) Concept, the Private (LEAST) Concept, and the Public (COMPOSITE) Concept. In most cases, the patterns of the three graphs are similar, with the COMPOSITE graph representing the net effect of the MOST and LEAST graphs. Therefore, we recommend using the COMPOSITE graph for interpretation throughout the instrument.

Some people, however, will find their MOST and LEAST graphs to be quite different. In these situations, the COMPOSITE graph still presents a reliable picture of the resulting behavioral style, and you will use it as your primary means to interpret the instrument. However, you will want to pay close attention to the patterns in your MOST and LEAST graphs as well.

Remember, the MOST graph describes the behavior that you feel is necessary for you to succeed. The LEAST graph describes your basic behavior—the way you are down deep. When a significant difference between the two graphs exists, you feel that to succeed, you must behave somewhat differently than you would "basically" choose to act. Even though you will use the COMPOSITE graph as your primary means of interpretation, as you work through the instrument, look at the explanations for the MOST and LEAST patterns as well. Doing so will help you understand the behavioral dynamics between these two graphs. *For more information on how to interpret differences between the MOST and LEAST graphs, please refer to page 146.*

DISCOVERING YOUR PREDOMINANT BEHAVIORAL STYLE

On the next two pages, we focus on the *general* aspects of the four behavioral tendencies—D, I, S, and C. Every personality contains all four elements. However, most of us find that one or perhaps two of the factors express themselves more strongly than others in our behavioral styles.

To discover your predominant element, find and circle the high point on your COMPOSITE graph on page 119. (In the example on the right, this person is a High S.) Then turn to pages 122 and 123 to read about your predominant factor. If your second highest point is near the highest, be sure to consider the overview for that characteristic as well. Over time, you will want to become familiar with the general descriptions of all four factors to understand and deal with others more effectively.

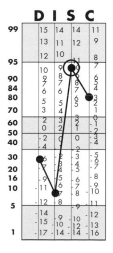

OVERVIEW OF BEHAVIORAL CHARACTERISTICS

DOMINANCE ("D")

Other Terms:	**Driver, Director**
Emphasis:	Controlling the environment by overcoming opposition to achieve desired goals
Key to Motivation:	Challenge
Basic Intent:	To *Overcome*

"D" quadrant people are self-starters who get going when things get tough. You thrive on competition and are usually direct, positive, and straightforward—sometimes blunt. You like to be center stage and in charge.

You will fight hard for what you think is the way to go but can accept momentary defeat without holding grudges. You hate routine and are prone to changing jobs, especially early in your career, until you find the challenge you need.

D's thrive on competition, tough assignments, heavy work loads, pressure, opportunities for individual accomplishment. You are discontented with the status quo.

You are a real individualist and very self-sufficient. You demand a great deal of yourself and others.

COMPLIANCE ("C")

Other Terms:	**Conscientious, Cautious, Analytical**
Emphasis:	Structuring the environment to produce products and services that meet high standards
Key to Motivation:	Protection/Security
Basic Intent:	To *Avoid Trouble*

The "C" quadrant person thrives on order, pre-determined methods, tradition, and conflict-free atmospheres with ample opportunity for careful planning and without sudden changes.

C methods are pre-determined, precise, and attentive to detail. You prefer to adapt to situations to avoid conflict and antagonism. Your need for self-preservation causes you to document everything that you do, and you try to do whatever others want you to do.

Naturally cautious, you prefer to wait and see which way the wind is blowing. Once your mind is made up, however, you can be very firm in adhering to procedures.

INFLUENCE ("I")

Other Terms:	**Expressive, Persuader**
Emphasis:	Creating the environment by motivating and aligning others to accomplish results.
Key to Motivation:	Recognition
Basic Intent:	To *Persuade*

"I" quadrant people thrive on social contact, one-on-one situations, and freedom from control and detail. I's are friendly, outgoing, persuasive, and confident.

Your basic interest is in people. You are poised and meet strangers well. People seem to respond to you naturally, and you usually have a wide range of acquaintances. Your innate optimism and people skills help you get along with most people, including competitors.

Often very fashionable dressers, I's join organizations for prestige and personal recognition.

STEADINESS ("S")

Other Terms:	**Amicable, Supporter**
Emphasis:	Maintaining the environment to carry out specific tasks.
Key to Motivation:	Appreciation
Basic Intent:	To *Support*

The "S" quadrant person thrives in a relaxed, friendly atmosphere without much pressure, one that offers security, limited territory, predictable routine, and credit for work accomplished.

You are usually amiable, easy-going, warm-hearted, home-loving, and neighborly. On the other hand, you may be undemonstrative and controlled. You conceal your feelings and sometimes hold a grudge.

Most of the time S people are even-tempered, low-key, emotionally mature, and unobtrusive. You are generally content with the status quo and prone to leniency with yourself and others.

S people dislike change. Once under way, you work steadily and patiently, and you dislike deadlines. You are usually very possessive and develop strong attachments for your things, your family, your department, your position.

Biblical **DISC**ernment® Inventory

STRENGTHS AND WEAKNESSES

Everyone's mix of behavioral tendencies contains both strengths and weaknesses. As author/consultant Peter Drucker points out, "the idea that there are 'well-rounded' people who have only strengths and no weaknesses . . . is a prescription for mediocrity, if not incompetence" (*Effective Executive, 72*). Rather than staff an organization to avoid weakness, suggests Drucker, companies should look for strengths in their people that will meet the demands of the situation.

When we concentrate on developing strengths rather than on avoiding weaknesses, we focus on what we *can* do, rather than what we *can't*, and play to those strong areas. As a result, our weaknesses become less influential in our behavior.

In order to do this, we must identify our own particular strengths and weaknesses and understand how they relate to each other. In many cases our weaknesses are actually the product of our strengths taken to the extreme. For example, perseverance can become stubbornness, or optimism can turn into over-confidence when pushed too far. In such instances, neutralizing a weakness can be as simple as exercising self-discipline.

When we understand ourselves and others thoroughly, we can learn how we work best and can then achieve our highest level of effectiveness. As we learn to answer the question, "What *can* I do?" rather than "What can I *not* do?", we feed the opportunity and starve the problem.

INSTRUCTIONS

Again, using your high factor that you identified on your COMPOSITE graph (page 119), locate the applicable lists below and on the facing page and check those Probable Strengths and Possible Weaknesses that you believe accurately describe you. If your profile reveals two equally high areas, choose descriptors from both lists.

THE "D"

PROBABLE STRENGTHS	POSSIBLE WEAKNESSES
❏ Decisive	❏ Overbearing
❏ Initiating	❏ Abrasive
❏ Forceful	❏ Impatient
❏ Assertive	❏ Blunt
❏ Competitive	❏ Demanding
❏ Goal-oriented	❏ Hasty
❏ Authoritative	❏ Dictatorial
❏ Independent	❏ Belligerent

THE "I"

PROBABLE STRENGTHS

- ❑ Charismatic
- ❑ Confident
- ❑ Gregarious
- ❑ Persuasive
- ❑ Participative
- ❑ Optimistic
- ❑ Stimulating
- ❑ Enthusiastic
- ❑ Communicative

POSSIBLE WEAKNESSES

- ❑ Impulsive
- ❑ Superficial
- ❑ Unrealistic
- ❑ Glib
- ❑ Overconfident
- ❑ Poor listener
- ❑ Self-centered
- ❑ Too trusting
- ❑ Emotional

THE "S"

- ☑ Self-controlled
- ❑ Accommodating
- ☑ Persistent
- ☑ Patient
- ☑ Good listener
- ☑ Easy-going
- ☑ Calm
- ☑ Sympathetic
- ☑ Warm
- ☑ Dependable

- ☑ Complacent
- ☑ Lenient
- ❑ Smug
- ❑ Indifferent
- ☑ Non-demonstrative
- ☑ Confrontation-averse
- ❑ Apathetic
- ❑ Plodding
- ☑ Passive
- ❑ Possessive

THE "C"

- ❑ Precise
- ❑ Adaptable
- ❑ Thorough
- ❑ Systematic
- ❑ Cautious
- ❑ Conscientious
- ❑ Orderly
- ❑ Well-prepared
- ❑ Accurate

- ❑ Too careful
- ❑ Obsessive/Compulsive
- ❑ Nit-picky
- ❑ Analysis paralysis
- ❑ Suspicious
- ❑ Finicky
- ❑ Detached
- ❑ Sensitive
- ❑ Indecisive

Biblical DISCernment® Inventory

INSTRUCTIONS FOR STRENGTHS AND WEAKNESSES GRAPHS

The lists on the previous two pages identify strengths and weaknesses that are characteristic of each of the four individual behavioral elements, D, I, S, and C.

Building on the lists, the graphs on pages 128 and 129 present a continuum of descriptive terms (strengths and weaknesses) that will help you better understand how strengths and weaknesses result from the interaction of these elements. The graph on page 128, when plotted according to your own particular combination of D, I, S, and C elements, will build your list of probable strengths, while the graph on page 129 will alert you to possible weaknesses.

PLOTTING THE GRAPHS

Copy the plotting points from your COMPOSITE graph on page 119 of this instrument onto the graphs on pages 128 and 129. Use the numbers on the left-hand side of each graph as reference points. Connect the plotting points just as you did on page 119 to duplicate the pattern. The graph patterns on pages 128 and 129 should be identical.

INTERPRETING THE GRAPHS

These graphs present two separate means of developing a comprehensive list of your strengths and the areas that need development. One method looks at the graph *patterns*, and the other takes into account the *relationship*, or the relative positions of the individual elements.

PATTERN

Notice that there is a continuum of descriptive terms under each letter. In each column, the words found between the plotting points for D, I, S, and C and the midline describe that individual's strengths or weaknesses. See the example at right, which is a Probable Strengths graph.

PROBABLE STRENGTHS

RELATIONSHIP

In addition to the *pattern* of the plotting points, the *relationship* between these points also indicates possible strengths and weaknesses. The *relationship* refers to combinations of factors *above* the midline and those *below* the midline. In this example, the appropriate relationships are D/S, D/C, I/S, and I/C. The descriptors for each relationship are shown in the corners of the graph. D is higher than S, so *gets results* applies. Because D is higher than C, *decisive* is an appropriate description. I is higher than both S and C, so the individual is likely to be both *personable* and *confident*.

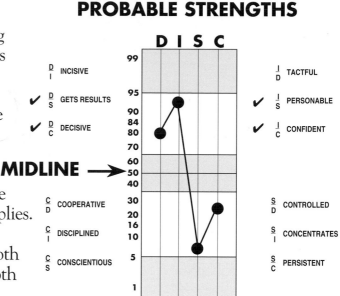

The procedure outlined in the above examples allows you to complete the graph on page 128 to determine your probable strengths caused by the interaction of the elements D, I, S, and C.

Follow the same steps using the graph on page 129 to identify your possible weaknesses.

IN SUMMARY

1. Plot your COMPOSITE graph from page 119 on both the strengths graph on page 128 and the weaknesses graph on page 129. The plotting points on the graphs should be identical.

2. Circle the descriptive terms according to both the pattern and the relationships that you believe accurately describe you.

3. Summarize your results as instructed on page 130.

PROBABLE STRENGTHS

D I S C

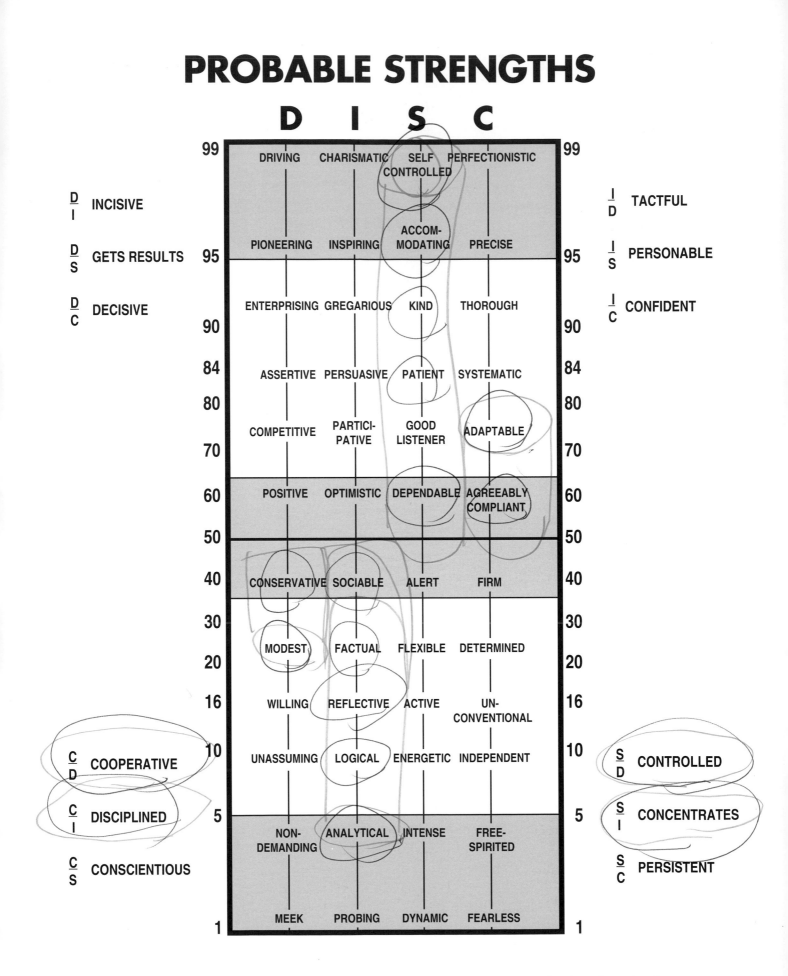

	D	I	S	C	
	DRIVING	CHARISMATIC	SELF CONTROLLED	PERFECTIONISTIC	99
$\frac{D}{I}$ INCISIVE					
$\frac{D}{S}$ GETS RESULTS	PIONEERING	INSPIRING	ACCOM-MODATING	PRECISE	95
$\frac{D}{C}$ DECISIVE	ENTERPRISING	GREGARIOUS	KIND	THOROUGH	90
	ASSERTIVE	PERSUASIVE	PATIENT	SYSTEMATIC	84 / 80
	COMPETITIVE	PARTICI-PATIVE	GOOD LISTENER	ADAPTABLE	70
	POSITIVE	OPTIMISTIC	DEPENDABLE	AGREEABLY COMPLIANT	60 / 50
	CONSERVATIVE	SOCIABLE	ALERT	FIRM	40 / 30
	MODEST	FACTUAL	FLEXIBLE	DETERMINED	20
	WILLING	REFLECTIVE	ACTIVE	UN-CONVENTIONAL	16
	UNASSUMING	LOGICAL	ENERGETIC	INDEPENDENT	10 / 5
	NON-DEMANDING	ANALYTICAL	INTENSE	FREE-SPIRITED	
	MEEK	PROBING	DYNAMIC	FEARLESS	1

Right side labels:

$\frac{I}{D}$ TACTFUL

$\frac{I}{S}$ PERSONABLE

$\frac{I}{C}$ CONFIDENT

$\frac{S}{D}$ CONTROLLED

$\frac{S}{I}$ CONCENTRATES

$\frac{S}{C}$ PERSISTENT

Left side labels:

$\frac{C}{D}$ COOPERATIVE

$\frac{C}{I}$ DISCIPLINED

$\frac{C}{S}$ CONSCIENTIOUS

POSSIBLE WEAKNESSES

D I S C

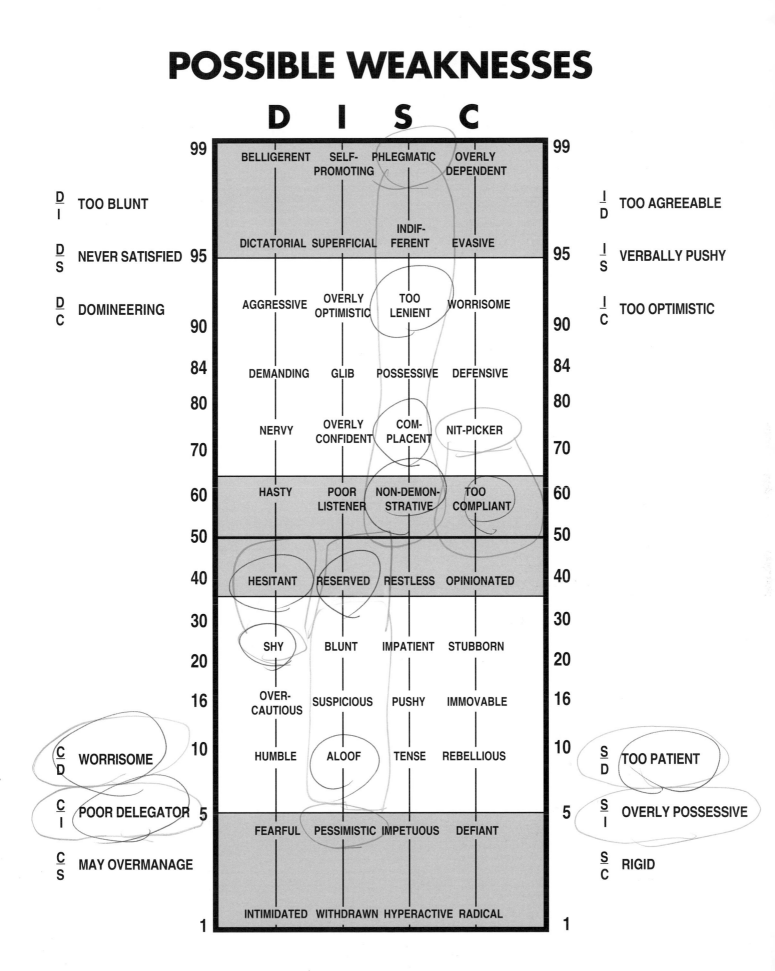

	D	I	S	C
99	BELLIGERENT	SELF-PROMOTING	PHLEGMATIC	OVERLY DEPENDENT
95	DICTATORIAL	SUPERFICIAL	INDIF-FERENT	EVASIVE
90	AGGRESSIVE	OVERLY OPTIMISTIC	TOO LENIENT	WORRISOME
84	DEMANDING	GLIB	POSSESSIVE	DEFENSIVE
70	NERVY	OVERLY CONFIDENT	COM-PLACENT	NIT-PICKER
60	HASTY	POOR LISTENER	NON-DEMON-STRATIVE	TOO COMPLIANT
40	HESITANT	RESERVED	RESTLESS	OPINIONATED
20	SHY	BLUNT	IMPATIENT	STUBBORN
16	OVER-CAUTIOUS	SUSPICIOUS	PUSHY	IMMOVABLE
10	HUMBLE	ALOOF	TENSE	REBELLIOUS
5	FEARFUL	PESSIMISTIC	IMPETUOUS	DEFIANT
1	INTIMIDATED	WITHDRAWN	HYPERACTIVE	RADICAL

Left-side labels:
- $\frac{D}{I}$ TOO BLUNT
- $\frac{D}{S}$ NEVER SATISFIED
- $\frac{D}{C}$ DOMINEERING
- $\frac{C}{D}$ WORRISOME
- $\frac{C}{I}$ POOR DELEGATOR
- $\frac{C}{S}$ MAY OVERMANAGE

Right-side labels:
- $\frac{I}{D}$ TOO AGREEABLE
- $\frac{I}{S}$ VERBALLY PUSHY
- $\frac{I}{C}$ TOO OPTIMISTIC
- $\frac{S}{D}$ TOO PATIENT
- $\frac{S}{I}$ OVERLY POSSESSIVE
- $\frac{S}{C}$ RIGID

SUMMARY

We have provided space below to summarize strengths, weaknesses, and behavioral tendencies you feel accurately describe you. Using the words checked in the lists on pages 124 and 125 as well as the words circled on the graphs on pages 128 and 129, develop a summary list below.

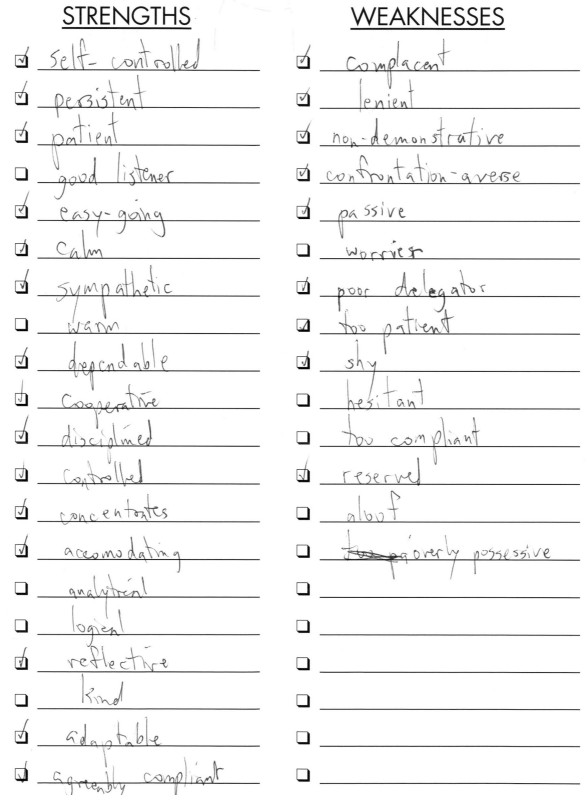

STRENGTHS	WEAKNESSES
☑ Self-controlled	☑ complacent
☑ persistent	☑ lenient
☑ patient	☑ non-demonstrative
☐ good listener	☑ confrontation-averse
☑ easy-going	☑ passive
☑ calm	☐ worrier
☑ sympathetic	☑ poor delegator
☐ warm	☑ too patient
☑ dependable	☑ shy
☑ cooperative	☐ hesitant
☑ disciplined	☐ too compliant
☑ controlled	☑ reserved
☑ concentrates	☐ aloof
☑ accomodating	☐ ~~too pa~~ overly possessive
☐ analytical	☐
☐ logical	☐
☑ reflective	☐
☐ kind	☐
☑ adaptable	☐
☑ agreeably compliant	☐

LEVERAGING STRENGTHS
AND DEFLECTING WEAKNESSES

1. Review your list of probable strengths on the facing page. Check the box next to each strength you believe that you use effectively in your current situation. What creative, short-range changes (6 months–1 year) can you make in your present situation to align more effectively with your strengths?

2. Identifying and acknowledging the presence of weaknesses is a key first step to growth. Review your list of possible weaknesses, and check those that you believe hinder your work and interpersonal effectiveness. Once you identify your weaknesses, here are several key strategies for dealing with them.

A. *Develop compensating skills:* Remember that the weaknesses on this list are not a handicap, but rather tendencies in our behavioral styles that we can control. For example, a naturally impatient person can *learn* to slow down and listen carefully to important information.

B. *Recognize your vulnerability and prepare for your behavior under stress:* Stress often brings our weaknesses to the surface. For example, impatience often becomes more pronounced in situations that demand great restraint. If we are alert both to our weaknesses and to the situations in which we experience stress, we can develop early warning systems that can help us neutralize the negative impact of these tendencies.

C. *Staff to your weaknesses:* Synergism flows from diversity. Identifying weaknesses alerts us to the need to surround ourselves with individuals and team members who are strong in those areas. The Apostle Paul writes, "Now God gives us many kinds of special abilities, but it is the same Holy Spirit who is the source of them all. There are different kinds of service to God, but it is the same Lord we are serving. There are many ways in which God works in our lives, but it is the same God who does the work in and through all of us who are His. The Holy Spirit displays God's power through each of us as a means of helping the entire church." I Corinthians 12:4–7 (TLB)

Biblical DISCernment® Inventory

INTERPRETING THE REPRESENTATIVE PROFILE PATTERNS

Every personality contains at least some degree of all four factors, even though some are high and others low. The particular ways in which the four factors combine and influence one another form a composite behavioral style.

As you might imagine, the potential variety of patterns is almost infinite and could threaten to overwhelm us. However, most behaviors tend to fall into broad groups of representative patterns from which you can choose the one that is closest to your own specific pattern.

On the following pages you will find descriptions and interpretations of the 17 representative patterns—four each for "D," "I," "S," and "C" personalities plus the Level patterns (page 143). In each quadrant, the particular pattern is characterized by *high* "D," "I," "S," or "C."

Using your COMPOSITE graph on page 119 of this instrument, find the pattern (page 133) that most closely matches it. Turn to page 134 to find what biblical character(s) matches your pattern. Write the pattern name and character that correspond to your profile below your graph on page 119, and then read the accompanying text for that pattern (pages 135–143) to learn more about your behavioral style. Each profile description includes information about that pattern's outstanding traits, the basic drives of the person who has that pattern, and areas in which that person might need to improve.

In addition, each profile describes at least one biblical model, with insights into how the biblical character responded to specific events. The final profile includes a description of Jesus' pattern to show how a person can be in balance with and controlled by the Holy Spirit.

What If I Don't See My Pattern?

Remember that these descriptions are based on large groups of people with behavioral tendencies represented by these patterns. Although it is unlikely that the interpretations will match your behavioral characteristics exactly, most people who use the Biblical **DISC**ernment® Inventory can find their own pattern or one that is close to it within the 17 representative DISC patterns. Those whose patterns are significantly different from the representative patterns can use behavioral relationships to interpret their patterns. Even if you found your pattern, you can use the behavioral relationships to gain additional insight about your behavioral style. Descriptions for each of the behavioral relationships begin on page 144.

How Will Knowing My Pattern Benefit Me?

The representative Biblical **DISC**ernment® Inventory patterns and interpretations are based on a *behavioral* profile only—without information about intelligence, personal values, versatility, and other factors that could affect your behavior. Again, no particular pattern is "good" or "bad," just as scoring high in one of the four DISC quadrants is not more desirable than a high score in another. Knowing your typical pattern should provide you with insights that will enable you to understand yourself and others in a way that maximizes your potential and your abilities.

REPRESENTATIVE BIBLICAL DISC PATTERNS

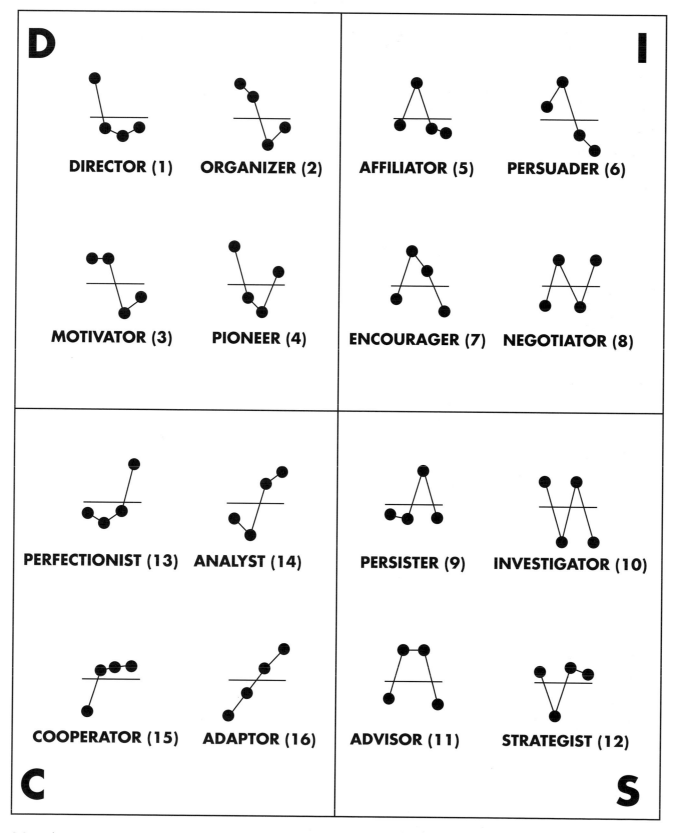

Biblical **DISC**ernment® Inventory

DISC HIGH STYLES AND BIBLICAL CHARACTERS

To associate a biblical character with a particular style, the authors conducted a detailed study to determine the specific traits or behavior of the individual as recorded in Scripture. When a character exhibited a consistent trait, we compared it with the descriptive terms on the DISC continuums. When a match occurs, it represents a Graph III, or PUBLIC view. In some cases, insufficient public information is available to make a confident match, and those biblical characters are indicated by asterisks (*) following their names.

DISC Blends	Biblical Model	Biblical Reference
1. **Director** (Primary "D")	Solomon	I Kings 10
2. **Organizer** (D/I)	Joshua, Sarah*	Joshua 24: 14–31; Gen. 16
3. **Motivator** (D=I)	Stephen, Laban, Lydia*	Acts 6; Gen. 29:15–30; Acts 16
4. **Pioneer** (D/C)	Paul, Rachel*	Gal. 2; Rom. 7:5–25; Gen. 30:1–24
5. **Affiliator** (Primary "I")	Aaron, King Saul	Ex. 4:14–17, 32:1–24; I Sam. 15
6. **Persuader** (I/D)	Peter, Rebekah	Acts 3 & 4; Luke 22; Gen. 24
7. **Encourager** (I/S)	Barnabas, Abigail	Acts 4:36–37, 9:26–27; I Sam. 25
8. **Negotiator** (I/C)	David, Mary Magdalene*	II Sam. 16, 18, 21; Ex. 15:20–21
9. **Persister** (Primary "S")	Isaac, Dorcas*	Gen. 26, 27; Acts 9:36–38
10. **Investigator** (S/D)	Nehemiah, Joseph, Martha*	Nehemiah 2, 3; Luke 10:38–42
11. **Advisor** (S/I)	Abraham, Hannah	Gen. 24, 16; I Sam. 1,2
12. **Strategist** (S/C/D)	Jacob, Anna*	Gen. 29–32; Luke 2:36–38
13. **Perfectionist** (Primary "C")	Luke, Esther	Luke 1:1–4; Esther 4, 5, 7
14. **Analyst** (C/S/D)	Moses, Thomas*, Naomi*	Ex. 3–4; John 20:24–28; Ruth 2, 3
15. **Cooperator** (C/I/S)	Elijah, Deborah*, Ruth*	I Kings 18, 19; Judges 4, 5; Ruth 3
16. **Adaptor** (C/S)	John, Mary*	John 19:26–27; Luke 1:26–56

Note: Tim LaHaye and Florence Littauer use the ancient four humours, "Choleric" (D), "Sanguine" (I), "Phlegmatic" (S), and "Melancholic" (C) to describe behavioral styles. Gary Smalley and John Trent use animal figures to represent the four styles: Lion (D), Otter (I), Golden Retriever (S), and Beaver (C).

(1) DIRECTOR—SOLOMON

OUTSTANDING TRAITS

- Aggressive, analytical, and independent.
- Driven to achieve goals, overcome obstacles.
- Welcomes responsibility; makes own decisions.
- Competitive; likes being in charge.

BASIC DRIVES

- Need to initiate action, exercise authority, and produce tangible results.
- Wants both power and freedom.
- Challenged by difficult problems that require brain-power, logic, and tactics.
- Desires fast-moving environment.

NEED FOR POSSIBLE IMPROVEMENT

- Can be cold, blunt, and critical.
- Impatient to get things done.
- Has difficulty with delegation and communication.
- Becomes easily bored with routine tasks.

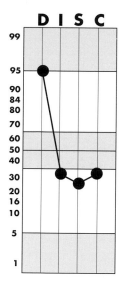

King Solomon typifies a Director's analytical, goal-driven, and independent style. His intuitive management skills and wisdom from God were strong factors in directing Israel to the pinnacle of its influence, and he himself became the richest and most widely sought after leader in the world. He possessed a unique understanding of difficult problems and acted quickly to solve them, as in his resolving a dispute between two women who both claimed to have given birth to the same baby (1 Kings 3).

Solomon, however, had difficulty in being accountable to others. In 1 Kings 11, God confronted him about not marrying foreign women who could lead him astray through unhealthy and unholy alliances. Rather than obey the Lord's direction, he decided to marry them and eventually he worshiped pagan gods. As a result, God removed Solomon's kingdom from his control and gave it to a subordinate.

In spite of this personal failure, we remember Solomon for developing a great kingdom and completing the writings of Proverbs, Song of Solomon and Ecclesiastes, all of which offer godly wisdom and practical insight for living a fulfilled life.

Like Solomon, a Director can accomplish much by assuming responsibility and initiating action to produce tangible results.

(2) ORGANIZER—SARAH, JOSHUA

OUTSTANDING TRAITS

- Aggressive, persuasive, active, and independent.
- Reluctant to give up or give in.
- Willing to take risks and implement bold plans.
- Friendly when things are going well, but tough when goals are blocked.

BASIC DRIVES

- Need for quick, measurable results.
- Loves competition and power; aspires to top roles.
- Desires fast-paced environment.
- Overcomes obstacles in pursuit of goals.

NEED FOR POSSIBLE IMPROVEMENT

- May be a poor delegator, direct but too brief communicator.
- Tends to listen half-heartedly.
- May neglect long-range planning.
- Impulsive in decision-making; shoots from the hip.

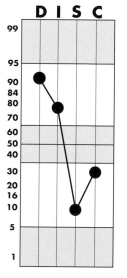

An Organizer's aggressive and persuasive abilities appear in the lives of Joshua and Sarah in the Old Testament. After Moses died, God chose Joshua to lead Israel into the promised land. His intense drive to achieve goals, regardless of obstacles, made him the logical commander to undertake this dangerous mission. He confidently led the army to many victories by organizing battle strategies, and his willingness to follow an unorthodox plan (Joshua 6) resulted in the conquest of Jericho.

Sarah, the wife of Abraham, was also an Organizer. She was willing to take risks and implement bold plans when faced with danger. In Genesis 12, when her husband's life was threatened in Egypt, she responded by agreeing to become a part of Pharaoh's household in order to save Abraham. Organizers, however, can be tough and impatient if anything stands in the way of reaching their goals, and if they do not achieve results quickly. When God's promise of a son to Abraham didn't happen in Sarah's time frame, she became impulsive and devised her own plan, involving her maid servant, Hagar. When Hagar became pregnant, Sarah demanded that Abraham take full responsibility for resolving the problem. In time, however, Sarah obeyed the Lord and bore Isaac, Abraham's promised heir. Like Sarah, Organizers should learn patience and listen to the counsel of others.

(3) MOTIVATOR—STEPHEN, LYDIA

OUTSTANDING TRAITS

- Verbally aggressive, outgoing, enthusiastic, and independent.
- Motivates and gets along well with a variety of people.
- Naturally persuasive, fluent speaker.
- Enjoys business and social activities that involve people.

BASIC DRIVES

- Equal desire to get results and to influence people.
- Demonstrates natural abilities through confidence and persuasion.
- Wants to change others, motivate them to accomplish and become.
- Desires prestige and status, recognition.

NEED FOR POSSIBLE IMPROVEMENT

- May overestimate ability to change people.
- Delegates well, but often weak in follow-through.
- Tendency to be too optimistic and oversell.
- May lean too heavily on own personality when dealing with others.

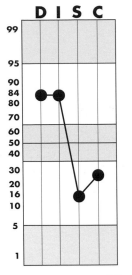

Stephen and Lydia are examples of Motivators who are outgoing and articulate. Stephen, one of the first church deacons, was best known for his eloquent speech and his ability for spirited debate. Acts 7 details a powerful sermon he delivered before the Sanhedrin council in which he gave bold testimony for Christ. Because of a Motivator's strong personality, however, others often feel intimidated by them, a situation that can cause intense disagreements. In the case of Stephen, his speech, although correct, so overwhelmed and angered the Sanhedrin, they stoned him to death.

Lydia was a Motivator who enjoyed challenges and was driven by an equal desire to achieve goals and influence people. Like a true Motivator, she enjoyed both business and social activities involving other people. She moved her cloth business from Asia to the European city of Philippi and was a successful businesswoman. After accepting Christ through the witness of the apostle Paul, she encouraged her whole family to follow her in belief and baptism. Afterward, Lydia was able to persuade Paul and Silas to stay in her home and start the first Christian church in Europe. Motivators should be cautious in over-extending their drive to change people. Not everyone needs to become a martyr like Stephen.

(4) PIONEER—PAUL

OUTSTANDING TRAITS

- Logical, factual, incisive, and systematic.
- Perfectionistic; not satisfied with just *any* answer.
- Challenged by problems requiring original and analytical effort.
- Decisive on routine matters; carefully weighs pros and cons on major issues.

BASIC DRIVES

- Equal striving for accomplishment and quality.
- Need to resolve perfectionism on the side of practical action.
- Prefers a changing environment.
- Wants authority and important assignments, advancement, and challenge.

NEED FOR POSSIBLE IMPROVEMENT

- Can be cool and blunt under pressure.
- Tends to be critical of others who don't meet their standards.
- Becomes impatient with routine.
- May appear indecisive when encountering a conflict between the big picture and attention to detail.

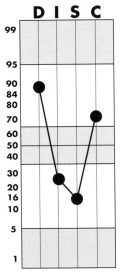

Pioneers respect direct, straightforward communication and appreciate solving problems that require an analytical effort. The Apostle Paul is a Pioneer who was challenged by problems requiring original and analytical thinking. He was logical, critical, and driven in advancing the Gospel. Paul is best known for understanding the significance of Christ's death on the cross and communicating the meaning of the freedom of God's grace versus the bondage of religious law. A pioneer in carrying the Good News to the Gentiles, his systematic skills were critical to planting churches throughout the Roman empire. Paul's commitment to providing right answers to problems resulted in being the author of 13 letters in the New Testament, each of which attempts to resolve important theological issues combined with practical action.

As a Pioneer, Paul enjoyed a good argument, seeing it as an intellectual challenge. His argumentative style often led to open disagreements with the Jewish leadership. Ultimately he was arrested, imprisoned, and martyred, partly due to his criticism of government leaders. Although Barnabas offset Paul's tendency for abruptness, the two separated when they disagreed over John Mark's failure to achieve Paul's standard of excellence. Pioneers like Paul often need to soften their intense impact and criticism of people.

(5) AFFILIATOR—AARON

OUTSTANDING TRAITS

- Outgoing, active, and independent.
- Optimistic, enthusiastic, and talkative.
- Tries to make a good first impression.
- Prefers to persuade rather than command.

BASIC DRIVES

- Wants popularity and prestige.
- Strives to make environment friendly and favorable.
- Desires group activities.
- Motivates others by teamwork and togetherness.

NEED FOR POSSIBLE IMPROVEMENT

- Can over-sell, over-talk, and over-commit.
- Too trusting; may misjudge others' capabilities.
- Impulsive; may jump to conclusions.
- Could improve on time management.

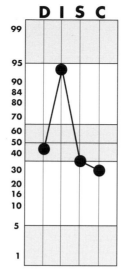

Aaron, an Affiliator, was active and outgoing, possessing excellent verbal skills. The Lord provided Aaron, an excellent and eloquent speaker, to be his brother Moses' mouthpiece when Moses felt inadequate to carry out his mission alone. Aaron's verbal skills and encouraging style proved to be particularly helpful to Moses in communicating God's message to the elders of Israel and Pharaoh. Affiliators also want to make any environment they are in favorable and friendly, at times trusting people too much and misjudging their motives and abilities. They have difficulty saying "no" and are often vulnerable to impulsive action without considering the consequences.

Aaron's tendency to avoid conflict and his need to get along with people created an unfortunate disaster described in Exodus 32. Unable to withstand the social pressures of the Israelite people, he gave in to them and approved the construction of a golden calf idol. When he was confronted by Moses, Aaron initially blamed the people rather than assuming personal responsibility for his actions but later recognized and repented. When controlled by the Holy Spirit, the Affiliator's self-confidence and optimism can motivate others to teamwork and togetherness.

(6) PERSUADER—PETER

OUTSTANDING TRAITS

- Energetic, positive, persuasive, and independent.
- Verbally dominates social and business situations.
- Goal-minded, direct action extrovert.
- Friendly, but argumentative and persistent.

BASIC DRIVES

- Control events and people.
- Self-motivated; thrives on taking risks.
- Convince others his/her way is right.
- Strong desire for acceptance.

NEED FOR POSSIBLE IMPROVEMENT

- May be too independent to change ways.
- Can be inconsiderate, stubborn, and argumentative.
- Needs to listen and observe more.
- Can be overly controlling.

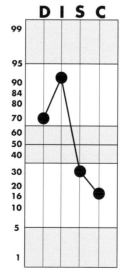

Peter illustrates the Persuader profile by his positive and persuasive social skills, combined with an uninhibited, action-oriented style. He acted spontaneously and did not mind taking risks. When the disciples suddenly saw Jesus walking on water (Matthew 14), Peter was the only one who stepped out of the boat and walked on the water with Jesus.

At times, Persuaders will show determination by attempting to control events and people. In the last days of Jesus' ministry on earth as He tried to prepare the disciples for his arrest, death, and resurrection (John 16), Peter tried to take charge of the situation. He took Jesus aside and rebuked Him, saying that he would never let this awful event happen to the Lord.

Persuaders want to know what they are being held accountable for and work best with clear instructions and few restrictions. In John 21, following the resurrection, Jesus instructs Peter about leading others to believe in Christ. Peter responded to the challenge and delivered an impromptu sermon in an outgoing and energetic style that led 3,000 people to profess their faith and follow Christ (Acts 2).

Those who deal with Persuaders should remember, however, that they prefer to focus on the big picture rather than on specific details.

(7) ENCOURAGER—ABIGAIL, BARNABAS

OUTSTANDING TRAITS

- Relaxed, friendly, understanding, and approachable.
- Optimistic; sees the potential in others despite their flaws.
- Empathetic listener; able to discern people's needs and provide practical solutions.
- Likeable, self-confident, and modest.

BASIC DRIVES

- Seeks to maintain harmony and peace.
- Driven to respond to the needs of others.
- Wants to encourage others through counsel and advice.
- Prefers a favorable, affirming environment.

NEED FOR POSSIBLE IMPROVEMENT

- May be overly accommodating in order to maintain relationships.
- May avoid confrontation and be too indirect in communication.
- Tends to be overly tolerant and too trusting.
- Focuses on people at the expense of tasks; may lose sight of important deadlines.

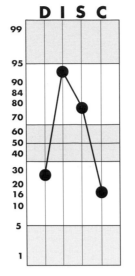

A relaxed, friendly, and approachable style characterizes Encouragers such as Barnabas and Abigail. People seek their counsel because they love people and are willing to listen. The name "Barnabas" means "son of encouragement " in Greek. Barnabas was always ready to help the needy and give people another chance. In Acts 9, when the disciples were afraid to associate with the recently converted Paul, Barnabas argued for Paul to be accepted. In conflict situations, Encouragers seek harmony and opportunities to be peacemakers.

Another Encourager, Abigail, (1 Samuel 25) is described as intelligent and practical. When her husband, Nabal, offended King David, she organized her servants to prepare a meal for David and his men. On her own initiative, she took the blame for the problem and asked the king to forgive Nabal. After averting the crisis, she returned home to find her husband drunk. The next morning, news of the previous evening's events so shocked Nabal that he had a heart attack and died. Abigail's devotion so impressed David that he later asked her to be his wife.

Encouragers should moderate a tendency to be overly tolerant and trusting when a more critical approach might lead to constructive change.

(8) NEGOTIATOR—DAVID

OUTSTANDING TRAITS

- Enthusiastic, active, and diplomatic.
- Cheerful, talkative, incurable optimist.
- Good conversationalist, at home with strangers.
- Smooth and low-pressure; creates atmosphere of goodwill.

BASIC DRIVES

- Need to be persuasive but careful of people's feelings.
- Seeks popularity, recognition, and acceptance.
- Wants to work for prestige organizations.
- Desires open, familiar, friendly surroundings.

NEED FOR POSSIBLE IMPROVEMENT

- May appear superficial and phony.
- Difficulty in being firm and direct.
- May subordinate results to relationships.
- May overestimate people's abilities.

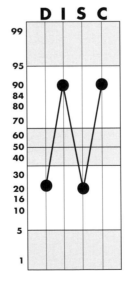

King David revealed the traits of a Negotiator by his tendency to being optimistic and cheerful as well as diplomatic and precise. Articulate, confident, and a skilled musician, he could create and maintain a pleasant atmosphere for himself and others. As a popular military leader, his men felt privileged to serve under him. He shared the limelight of victories with his troops and enjoyed being with them. In general, Negotiators respond best in the role of a diplomat, rather than that of a dictator, and achieve success when having opportunities to show good will to others.

A Negotiator represents two incongruent behavioral styles: positive optimism with cautious introspection. These two opposite drives caused great emotional changes in David which at times made it difficult to control. Under stress, feelings took precedence over logic. In 2 Samuel 11, King David became involved in an adulterous relationship with Bathsheba, the wife of one of his officers. When the relationship led to a pregnancy and an illegitimate child, he tried to cover-up his actions by a plot that included deceit and murder. Faced with the consequences of his action, David repented and returned to fellowship with God. Psalms 51 and 32 give a private account of his feelings during these events, advocating honest confession as the best response to compromise and failure.

(9) PERSISTER—ISAAC, DORCAS

OUTSTANDING TRAITS
- Modest, sociable, dependable, and determined.
- Steady, consistent; prefers one project at a time.
- Likes specialized areas of endeavor.
- Patient and controlled; reacts negatively to change.

BASIC DRIVES
- Strives to maintain the status quo.
- Prefers a few close, intimate relationships.
- Wants predictable work environment, opportunity to specialize.
- Emphasizes persistence and dependability.

NEED FOR POSSIBLE IMPROVEMENT
- Can conceal grievances; hold grudges.
- Slow to take initiative.
- Difficulty adapting to change.
- May have low sense of urgency.

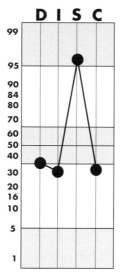

Isaac and Dorcas demonstrate Persister characteristics by their moderate, consistent, and dependable behavior, characterized by patience and control. Isaac worked patiently in his father's fields until he was 40 before meeting and marrying Rebekah, and the two maintained family and friendship ties at home.

Persisters want peace and harmony, and avoid confrontation if possible. When Isaac followed God's instructions to settle in the land of Gerar and became very wealthy, the Philistines, envious of his success, tried to intimidate him by destroying his wells. Rather than confronting them, Isaac moved his family to other lands. Persisters would benefit from learning how to face conflict and adjust quickly to change.

Persisters are intensely loyal, preferring to work behind the scenes with associates who express sincere interest in them. For example, in the New Testament, a woman named Dorcas was a faithful disciple who continually performed deeds of kindness and charity, making clothes for the needy in the community. When Dorcas died suddenly (Acts 9), her friends experienced intense grief about her loss. Peter, in a demonstration of God's power, raised her from the dead, to the great joy of those around her. This miracle shows how Persisters evoke deep affection and attachment from friends and associates.

(10) INVESTIGATOR—MARTHA, NEHEMIAH

OUTSTANDING TRAITS
- Determined, logical, tenacious, and independent.
- Friendly but aloof; deliberate and thorough.
- Dispassionately objective; digs for facts; chases clues.
- Results-oriented without a sense of urgency.

BASIC DRIVES
- Basically suspicious and skeptical; looks for hidden meanings.
- Challenged by tough problems.
- Likes to work independently at own pace.
- Prefers working with things rather than people.

NEED FOR POSSIBLE IMPROVEMENT
- Sees people as annoying obstructions.
- Can be blunt, tactless, stubborn, and obstinate.
- Difficult to change his/her mind.
- Needs help in persuading and motivating others.

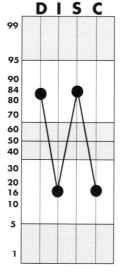

Nehemiah and Martha depict Investigators' tendencies: determined, logical, and tenacious. Perhaps an Investigator's greatest strength is the ability to analyze problems and evaluate action steps objectively. Nehemiah administered the affairs of the Jews while they lived in the promised land. His task-oriented skills enabled him to rebuild the walls of Jerusalem in just 52 days even though he faced stiff opposition. Investigators may have difficulty persuading others to accept their sense of urgency in assuming tasks. When faced with opposition, they tend to jump to suspicions rather than to conclusions.

In the New Testament, Martha, the sister of Lazarus and Mary, was able to organize tasks in a systematic, deliberate manner. Martha invited Jesus (Luke 10) and His disciples to dine in her home, determined to provide the best in hospitality. On the other hand, her sister, Mary, was more interested in talking with Jesus than in complying with Martha's action plan. As Mary sat at Jesus' feet, Martha's frustration boiled over, and she asked Jesus to tell Mary to help her prepare the meal. Jesus, however, affirmed Mary's actions and exhorted Martha not to be upset. Although Investigators accomplish much by their hard work and dedication, they should balance their commitment to tasks with sensitivity to the needs and feelings of others.

(11) ADVISOR—ABRAHAM, HANNAH

OUTSTANDING TRAITS

- Easy-going, friendly, relaxed, and warm.
- Extremely likeable and non-threatening.
- Approachable, good-listener, and patient.
- Poised and self-confident, devoted and loyal.

BASIC DRIVES

- Need to demonstrate amiability and goodwill.
- Must be with people, not alone.
- Driven to teach, counsel, and advise.
- Prefers an unhurried, favorable environment.

NEED FOR POSSIBLE IMPROVEMENT

- Too easy with marginal workers.
- Difficulty giving direct orders.
- May hold grudges.
- Can be indecisive in dealing with others.

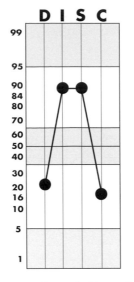

Abraham and Hannah exemplify Advisor qualities: amiable, practical, and down-to-earth. They are also patient, empathetic, and considerate when dealing with others. Genesis 13 describes how Abraham responded when strife arose between his herdsmen and his nephew Lot's workers. His solution was to separate the two groups by giving Lot the first choice of land to settle on, preventing further conflict and restoring peace in their family relationship.

Advisors respond positively to those in authority and follow through well on tasks assigned to them. Abraham faced the ultimate test of loyalty by placing the future of Isaac, his first-born, in God's hands after God asked Abraham to offer Isaac as a sacrifice.

Advisors are uncomfortable with conflict. When Hannah (1 Samuel 1) faced ridicule from relatives because of her inability to bear children, she internalized her feelings, resulting in years of personal struggle and depression. Hannah finally committed this conflict to God and vowed that if she could bear children, she would dedicate her first-born to a life of service to God. God responded, and after the birth of Samuel, Hannah faithfully fulfilled her promise. Advisors make valuable contributions through dedicated service. They particularly appreciate those who show sincere interest in them. The actions of both Abraham and Hannah illustrate what happens when a person places complete faith and trust in the Lord.

(12) STRATEGIST—JACOB

OUTSTANDING TRAITS

- Positive, cool, systematic, and steady.
- Direct; tells it like it is.
- Challenged by difficult analytical problems.
- Patient, controlled, moderate and deliberate.

BASIC DRIVES

- Equal desire to achieve and to be right.
- Maintain status quo; avoid unnecessary risk or trouble.
- Wants to work on one thing at a time
- Prefers facts, figures, and things to working with people.

NEED FOR POSSIBLE IMPROVEMENT

- Tends to hold grudges, get even.
- Difficulty in communicating effectively with others.
- Needs help juggling multiple projects.
- Never completely satisfied.

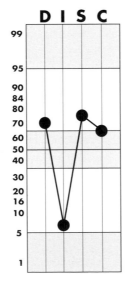

Jacob is described as a Strategist because of his steady and straightforward approach to life. Determined and direct, once he set his sights on a goal he tended to be unrelenting in achieving it. Genesis 29 chronicles how Jacob met and fell in love with his uncle Laban's daughter, Rachel. The condition for marrying her was that Jacob serve for seven years tending Laban's livestock. Jacob ended up working for his uncle for 20 years. During this time, Laban made many promises to Jacob which were continually broken. But Jacob persevered, finally taking Rachel as his wife.

Rather than quickly responding to aggressive people, Strategists tend to internalize conflict and remember wrongs done to them. They are not apt to show hurts openly, have a tendency to bear grudges and, in time, try to get even. Although Jacob persevered through the years of deception (Genesis 31), they experienced ongoing conflict, and Jacob deceived Laban about his intent to move his family. After some intense strife, they ultimately responded to God, settled their dispute, and restored harmony.

Rarely are Strategists satisfied when striving for quality. In fact, others often think of them as perfectionists. Understanding their preference for working alone rather than interacting with people should cause colleagues to moderate their expectations of personal support while working with Strategists.

(13) PERFECTIONIST—LUKE, ESTHER

OUTSTANDING TRAITS

- Conservative, logical, and conscientious.
- Precise and accurate; a stickler for details.
- Diplomatic and tactful; alert to hidden meanings and ulterior motives.
- Restless and discontented; strives for perfection.

BASIC DRIVES

- Needs to feel he or she is doing the right thing.
- Wants to avoid unnecessary risk or trouble, to be careful and cooperative.
- Prefers to follow the rules.
- Needs to know exactly what is expected, so he or she can do it thoroughly and well.

NEED FOR POSSIBLE IMPROVEMENT

- May spend too much time doing things alone to be sure they're right.
- Checking and re-checking details may hinder performance.
- May appear indecisive in search of perfect solution.
- Desire to please may inhibit actions and results.

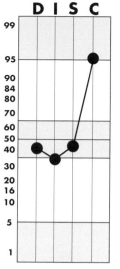

Precise, reliable, and tactful, Luke and Esther offer clear examples of the Perfectionist pattern. People see them as conscientious in following directives, sticklers for details, and factual when giving descriptions. Luke, a physician, carefully documents the perfect humanity of the Son of Man and details Jesus' ancestry, birth, and early life before describing His earthly ministry. Since Luke did not witness the events of Christ's life, he affirms his drive for accuracy by stating in the gospel's introduction: "Since I myself have carefully investigated everything from the beginning, it seemed good also to me to write an orderly account for you."

Perfectionists can be diplomatic on one hand and discontented on the other. Their precise checking and re-checking of details may combine to inhibit decisive action. Queen Esther could not ignore a plot to eliminate the Jewish people, even though she could not predict the King's reaction to her intervention. She agonized over the best approach to appeal to her husband on the Jewish people's behalf. Her carefully crafted plan ultimately revealed a deadly plot and focused the wrath of the King on the real traitors. Her action averted the annihilation of the Jewish nation. The alert and logical approach of a Perfectionist can have lasting impact in the lives of others.

(14) ANALYST—MOSES, THOMAS

OUTSTANDING TRAITS

- Reliable, factual, steady, and cooperative.
- Painstakingly accurate; incisive in approach to attaining goals.
- Diplomatic and precise; avoids unnecessary risk or trouble.
- Sensitive to possible hidden meanings and ulterior motives.

BASIC DRIVES

- Challenged by difficult problems that require logical thought and analysis.
- Driven to find the *right* answer.
- Wants to be part of a team.
- Likes standard operating procedures, system, and order.

NEED FOR POSSIBLE IMPROVEMENT

- May be too dependent upon procedures.
- Tendency to spend too much time checking and re-checking details.
- Decisions are apt to be tentative and low-risk.
- May hesitate to act without orders, rules, or precedent.

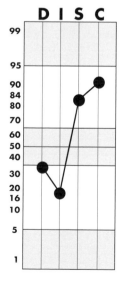

Moses and Thomas exemplify the characteristics of an Analyst: factual, steady, reliable, and committed to maintaining high standards, expecting others to live up to the same creed. Moses exhibited these traits (Exodus 3) after he was commissioned to represent the Lord before Pharaoh and attempt to lead God's people out of Egyptian bondage. He spent a lot of time questioning God, checking and rechecking the details of His plan. Like most Analysts, he was tentative, guarded and hesitant to act without clear orders. Once Moses was totally assured of God's plan, he took his brother, Aaron, and communicated God's warnings to Pharaoh.

Because Analysts are logical and critical, they make decisions based on proven precedent and known facts. In John 20, Thomas questioned the account of the disciples who reported seeing the resurrected Christ, stating that unless he could see and touch the nail scars of Jesus, he could not believe their claims. Thomas' doubts were not out of disrespect, but out of a deep desire to know and verify the facts. He quickly proclaimed Jesus as Lord following his time with the resurrected Christ. A commitment to analyzing the truth is a valuable trait can demonstrate honesty and open-mindedness rather than doubt.

(15) COOPERATOR—RUTH, ELIJAH

OUTSTANDING TRAITS

- Modest, sociable, predictable, and cooperative.
- Steady under most pressures; reacts negatively to changes.
- Directs skills into areas requiring depth and specialization; prefers dealing with one project at a time.
- Poised and cordial; can create and maintain atmosphere of goodwill.

BASIC DRIVES

- Nature is to conserve rather than expand.
- Minimize risks by careful investigation.
- Wants to please and stabilize the environment.
- Prefers atmosphere free of conflict and complications.

NEED FOR POSSIBLE IMPROVEMENT

- Unaggressive; may minimize risks by putting things off.
- May dawdle and deliberate before deciding.
- Tends to be too conventional vs. innovative.
- Easily hurt by being too trusting.

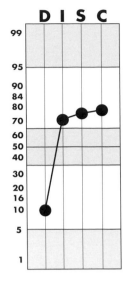

As Cooperators, Ruth and Elijah were sociable, steady, and conscientious. Poised and cordial, Ruth cooperated with Naomi's plan (Ruth 3) to appeal to Naomi's kinsman, Boaz, to develop a personal relationship with him. Ruth carried out the plan with grace and character, so impressing Boaz that he ultimately took Ruth as his wife.

When faced with challenges, Cooperators are intense and can be counted on to set up procedures with which to confront them successfully. I Kings 18 details how God instructed Elijah to challenge a group of 450 prophets of Baal. Like a true Cooperator, he prepared a detailed plan to bring down these false prophets. The plan succeeded and destroyed of all the prophets of Baal.

Cooperators can be hurt by rejection or rebuff. They desire harmony and a life free of antagonism. As a result of Elijah's destroying the false prophets, Jezebel declared her intention to track Elijah down and kill him. Afraid, Elijah fled the land, in a depression so intense that he wanted to take his own life. But the Lord understood Elijah's pain and responded with support and sensitivity to his condition.

Cooperators need to exercise caution, because their drive to please can lead to misunderstandings and hurt. Cooperators need to face problems and personal conflicts squarely and to take responsible and constructive action.

(16) ADAPTOR—JOHN, MARY

OUTSTANDING TRAITS

- Conservative, reserved, stable, and conscientious.
- Accommodating, precise, courteous, and systematic.
- Passion for impeccability and order.
- Follows directions carefully.

BASIC DRIVES

- Plans ahead to avoid risk or trouble.
- Needs to follow orders, precedent, rules and regulations.
- Likes to work as member of a team.
- Prefers to work with things vs. people.

NEED FOR POSSIBLE IMPROVEMENT

- Difficulty in delegation; tends to overmanage.
- May give in to avoid antagonism.
- Waits for instructions before acting.
- Spends too much time checking and rechecking.

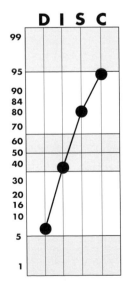

Adaptors hesitate to act on their own initiative, waiting and responding to instructions given by their authority. People generally view them as conservative, accommodating, and stable.

An Adaptor's cooperative, conscientious and contemplative style is found in both Mary and John. Their need for structure and order often led them to ask detailed questions to clarify instructions for tasks given to them in their service to God. The angel Gabriel met Mary and explained that she had been chosen to give birth to God's Son, the long-awaited Messiah (Luke 1). The record states that she asked specific and detailed questions concerning how that could be possible, since she was a virgin. After receiving an explanation of God's plan, Mary's response was one of total submission and cooperation in compliance with God's plan.

Because Adaptors are among the most loyal of all people, they strongly value close family relationships. The gospel of John (19) records that John, the Beloved, was the only disciple who remained at the cross when Christ was crucified. Jesus specifically instructed him to take care of Mary, His mother, after He was gone. Like a responsible Adaptor, John gladly accepted the assignment and faithfully fulfilled his mission.